THE MONA LISA SISTERS

GEORGE CRAMER

A Russian Hill Press Book
United States • United Kingdom • Australia

R
H
P Russian Hill Press

ISBN: 9781734122060 (softcover)
ISBN: 9781734122077 (eBook)

Library of Congress Control Number: 2020903672

Cover Design by Beatrice Morales

Dedicated to the memory of
Lura Grisham Myer, my grandmother.

THE MONA
LISA SISTERS

ONE

New Year's 1894 was not the happiest day of my life.

I was born Lura Grisham in 1870 to George and Elizabeth Grisham in the rural town of Ridgefield, Connecticut. Beginning with a modest inheritance, Father built a small railroad connecting Connecticut and the city of New York. He prospered and became one of the wealthiest men in America. My home from birth has been Grisham Manor. Father built it to be the most exquisite summer home, not just in Fairfield County, but in all Connecticut. Mother loved it so much that it became the family's year-round home.

The manor house, situated on twenty-eight acres atop a small knoll, gives us a view of the town from the veranda and dining room. The three-story Queen Anne contains sixteen rooms. Painted a pastel yellow, it exudes warmth and comfort. My bedroom for the first twelve years of my life was on the second floor, next to my parents' suite. Designed as a nursery, it had spacious accommodations. Aside from their magnificent master suite, my parents had hoped to fill the five other bedrooms with children. Alas, it wasn't to be. My birth was difficult for Mother and resulted in her never again being able to conceive.

On my twelfth birthday, dissatisfied with being confined to the nursery, I moved, without permission, to the third floor. Leaving my childish furniture behind, I claimed ownership of the room's lovely Elizabethan furniture. Father thought it funny. Mother, at first furious, soon forgave me. I chose the modest-sized tower room because it permitted me a view of the town and much of the valley. Beyond the manor and several farms, the road from the county seat wound south to New York.

I remember our old Methodist Episcopal Church before it burned down. It was tall, three stories plus a steeple. I could see the roof and bell tower from my window. Father once told me the spire helped people look up to the heavens. The tallest building in town, the roof was slate gray and the walls white. The first-floor walls were built of red bricks; the other floors were wood. I could not see it from my window, but there was a small parsonage on the property. When the church burned, it was spared. During the fire, the afternoon breeze carried smoke and soot across the fields. Standing in my room, the window open, I could see ashes and smell the awful

8

odor of fire. We suffered for weeks afterward as the acrid stench of the residue drifted in on the wind. The odious remnant made all the worse by the turpentine and linseed oil used for decades on the church floors. The new church was not as tall as the old one, and except for the wooden steeple, built of brick.

Ridgefield wasn't much more than a village then. The Roman Catholics had a small church on the outskirts, near Bartolini's Mercantile.

The one drawback to my tower room was that I could not see the carriage entry. I couldn't identify visitors without leaving my room. If I heard a coach arrive, I had to go down the stairs, hurry to the front, and join Mother as she greeted the guests.

Breakfast was usually in the nook off the kitchen. Like my tower room two stories above, the small area was octagonal with windows in every direction except for the doorway to the kitchen. I'm sure my father designed it that way so he could enjoy his morning coffee regardless of the season. It also gave him a chance to visit with the household staff. Father came from working stock and never treated the hired help as anything other than his equal.

When our church was rebuilt after the fire, Father bought two Mason and Hamlin pump organs. He donated one to our church and the other to the Roman Catholic Church where his Irish railroad workers worshiped. Father told me that many of the Irish had been enslaved in much the same manner as the Negro.

"Lura, our treatment of the Negro and the Irish has been only slightly better than the way we treat the Indian."

"What do you mean?"

"Many still believe that the Irish and the Negro are no better than work animals and that all Indians should be wiped from the land."

"Father, that's terrible."

"I know. We must treat everyone with respect and an open heart. You must never forget we are all God's children."

My father and mother had no living relatives. Father was one of six children, all boys. His parents and brothers died of cholera when he was five. He was raised by a freed family slave and supported by the proceeds from the sale of the family's landholdings. Like me, Mother was an only child. Her father, a Union officer, died at Gettysburg, her mother, the year I was born.

TWO

I FIRST MET WALTER MYER, ONE OF MY FATHER'S engineers, who designed railway bridges, when he came to Grisham Manor for dinner. I was twenty, an age that found most single women on the path to spinsterhood. Six-foot-tall, he had unruly chestnut brown hair. Not the most handsome man I had ever met, he exuded strength and warmth. His eyes were unusual. When we met, I assumed they were hazel. My thought dispelled when I visited Father at his office a few days later. Walter and he were talking outside. In the natural light, they were green with flecks of gold. I had never seen such eyes.

It was what romantics often refer to as love at first sight. I knew that one day I would marry him. From then on, I managed to find a reason to visit Father's office two or three times a month. I doubt that either Walter or Father had the slightest inkling that I was enamored.

Walter was an excellent engineer whom Father had come to rely on more as the years passed. At first, an occasional dinner guest, his visits became more regular as the railroad grew.

Mother was the first to realize I harbored feelings for him. One day she confronted me. "Do you love him?"

"Yes, with all my heart."

"Oh, child, what shall we do? Does he know how you feel?"

I didn't know if he did; I doubted it. I had to confess that I had never been alone with him or even had a serious conversation with him.

"We'll tell Father and see what he thinks."

"Can you do it? I don't know what to say."

Mother saw my fear and understood how naïve I was in the ways of men and love.

"I'll talk to Father."

MOTHER TOLD ME WHEN FATHER INQUIRED IF perchance Walter held any interest in me, he was taken aback. "Mr. Grisham, I have admired Lura for some time now."

"Why haven't you made your intentions known to Lura or me?"

"Sir, I feared that you might think I was interested in her for your fortune. Nor did I believe Lura could have any interest in me, a simple bridge builder."

"How could you think that I would object to you courting my daughter?"

Mother told me that she and Father thought our marriage destined for early and sure success. It wasn't so simple for us. I knew I was in love with him, but we needed to know one another better before we took steps towards marriage. Walter's dinner visits at Grisham Manor became a weekly occurrence. At first, he and Father would retire to Father's office after the meal, where they sipped brandy and smoked cigars.

Finally exasperated, I confronted my father in his study.

"Lura, what's on your mind? You seem hesitant about something," Father said after several minutes of casual conversation.

"Father, it appears to me that you're courting Walter."

"Courting? Whatever do you mean?"

"Think about it."

"What? Mother and I have him for dinner as often as seemly."

"True, but after dinner, you and he retire to your study, drink brandy, and enjoy your cigars until well past a decent hour." I paused so as not to show my frustration. "You might consider allowing us some time together."

Father was aghast, "I'm beyond sorry. I didn't realize—"

"You should have."

"It will not happen again," he said after an embarrassed silence, followed by a gentle embrace.

After my conversation with Father, Walter and I began sitting on the veranda and talking. As I came to know him and his plans to help Father grow the railroad, the more I became sure he was the man I was to marry.

As winter became spring followed by summer, Walter came early for Sunday dinners, and we took carriage rides. The air in Connecticut during the summer is filled with the sweet aroma of Indian corn and alfalfa. Our drives took us beyond town and occasionally as far as New York's state line. Whenever we crossed into that state, we talked of the day we would travel to New York City and its vast harbor. From there we would board one of the transatlantic steamers bound for France. "We'll honeymoon in Paris," became our shared dream.

On the return rides, we frequently stopped to visit my best friend, Emily Bartolini, at Bartolini's Mercantile. Emily and I would look at the catalogs for the latest Paris fashions while Walter and Mr. Bartolini enjoyed a cigar and talked politics. It was on one of these rides that we first kissed. It was awkward for me. I felt as though I had failed my first test as a woman. Walter didn't tell me, then or ever, where he learned to kiss, but he assured me that I had a knack for it.

Time seemed to drag. I was afraid he would never formally ask me to marry him. I need not have worried. Walter asked Father for my hand in marriage at our 1892 Thanksgiving dinner. Mother took over once Father gave his permission, and I accepted Walters's proposal. She told me men have no sense when it comes to women, no matter how successful they are in business or industry.

"We'll have an engagement party over the Christmas holidays. You're not to announce the engagement until then, not even to your friends."

Walter and I agreed, with the proviso that we would not wait the traditional year before marrying. Mother accepted the compromise.

"All right, but you must wait until spring. Father and I were married on April seventeenth. It would please us if you married on our anniversary."

"That will make us very happy." Father beamed.

Feeling happiness such as I had never experienced, I took Walter's large hands into mine, "Will that please you, my husband-to-be?"

"Whatever pleases you, my wife-to-be."

It was settled. We would marry on their anniversary, and all would be well.

MY PARENTS, THEIR PARENTS, AND THEIR PARENTS were all Methodist Episcopalians. Walter was Catholic. After much prayer and contemplation, I told Walter and my parents that I would convert to Catholicism. All three refused to accept my wish to change beliefs, and I remained in the traditional family religion.

The four of us, sincere Christians, were liberal in our approach to organized religion. We neglected to mention to Pastor Carter that both Walter and Emily Bartolini, my maid of honor, were Catholic. Thus, we became husband and wife on my parents' anniversary. We had a beautiful memory we could share and celebrate with Mother and Father.

We slept that first night in my bedroom. I was terrified that I would let Walter down. As our wedding night progressed, I became positive that virginity was one other thing we had in common. Our awkwardness didn't last long as we shared newly discovered delights.

We left the next morning for New York, where we enjoyed a short honeymoon. While planning our wedding, we had talked about travel to Paris. We postponed the trip because Walter was overseeing the completion of a bridge connecting the tracks between Philadelphia and Chicago And my father could not spare him. "I understand. Remember, I'm the daughter of a railroad man. We'll go next year on our anniversary," I assured my husband.

Upon our return from New York, Mother said Father was ecstatic. He had long hoped we would marry, and that Walter would someday take over the business. We rented a small cottage in Ridgefield. Walter drew plans for a home of our own on the hill next to Grisham Manor, a house that would never be our home.

By Independence Day, Mother knew I was with child. I didn't tell her, she told me.

"How can I be?" I gasped. "We just got married."

"Have you missed your monthly time?"

"I may have." I hadn't thought about it. My time wasn't always regular.

"May have?" Mother said with a laugh. "What a child you are. Tell me when the last time was."

I thought for a moment before looking up in shock. "Why, Mother, I do believe the last time was in April, the week after the wedding. I remember because I was so frightened that it would come upon me on the seventeenth."

"That is three months, darling."

"Oh, Lord, I'm with child," I gasped and added, "whatever shall I do?"

"First, let's go see Dr. Stevens."

Dr. Stevens confirmed our suspicions. "Unless I'm mistaken, the baby should arrive in late January."

That evening I waited until we were in bed before telling Walter. The happiest couple in the world, we counted our blessings. We had each other, our first child would be born in six months, and next year we would travel to Paris for the summer. By the time we returned, the home of our dreams would be ready for Walter Myer and family.

We were blessed.

The next three months of my pregnancy progressed normally. As our child grew, so did my wardrobe. Emily Bartolini would be the godmother, and once again, Pastor Carter had to look the other way. By the middle of the seventh month, my stomach looked like one of those Civil War observation balloons. I was having such a miserable time that Mother insisted we move out of the rental cottage and into Grisham Manor, at least until the baby arrived.

The servants were happy to have me back, and I loved being with them. Each morning, I made my way to the breakfast nook to share coffee with Father. My life was perfect with Father, Mother, and Walter looking after me. One morning in October, Father didn't come down.

"Have you seen Father?" I asked Cook.

"No, Missy Lura, I haven't. I'm worried. Mister George never misses his morning coffee."

I sent for Walter. "Something's wrong. Father hasn't come down this morning. Please come with me to his room."

I knocked on Father's door. "Father, it's me. Are you alright?" I repeated my query, but there was still no response.

"Please, Walter, see to Father."

"George. George, are you there?" Walter knocked and receiving no answer, opened the door, stepped in, and closed it behind him.

It was but a moment but seemed a lifetime before he came back. From the look of devastation, I knew that Father was dead.

"He looks peaceful. He must have died in his sleep."

Taking me by the hand, Walter brought me to my father's side. I fainted. Walter caught me. When I woke, he was sobbing. He was as close to my father as any son could have been.

He was the first to speak. "We have to tell your mother."

"I'll do it. You stay with Father."

I went through the sitting room that divided my parent's bedchambers. Mother was sitting up as I entered the room. She was beaming.

"Why, good morning, Darling. This is a pleasant surprise."

When she saw my face, I'm sure Mother knew that Father was gone. She collapsed and fell back on the bedcover, convulsing with sobs as tears fell from her tightly closed eyes. I went to her. Taking her into my arms, I rocked her like a child. Neither of us uttered a word for long minutes.

"I have to see him. Is Walter here?"

"Yes, Mother. He's with Father."

"Ask him to come to me. I may need to lean on him. Please get me a dressing gown."

When I returned with Walter, Mother was at her dressing table, combing out her hair with slow and deliberate strokes. Tears were visible on her cheeks.

"Give me a moment to finish my hair. I don't want to look a mess." Once finished putting her hair up, she rose and said, "Now, I'm ready. Walter, please help me to George's room." At the door to his room, she said, "You can both leave me now. I wish to be alone with Father. Walter, please go to the parsonage and ask Pastor Carter to come." Mother stepped into Father's room. In the time that she lived after Father died, I never again saw her cry.

The funeral, held three days later, brought dignitaries from as far away as Washington, D.C. It was the largest funeral I ever attended. Mother insisted that the servants sit with the family.

A few months after Father's death, I had concerns about Mother. "Walter, she isn't herself. I can't get her to talk about Father."

"She worries me as well, and she's not eating."

"She never wants to leave the bedroom suite. Every time I go in, she seems to be writing. When she sees me, she puts whatever it is in the desk drawer. She hasn't left the house since the funeral."

THREE

THANKSGIVING WAS A TIME FOR CELEBRATION IN our home. Rarely was anyone outside the family or household staff invited. Walter had been an exception. Mother always worked with the servants to decorate the house. Grisham Manor's dining room was unique in construction and ornamentation. With Tiffany windows, ten-foot ceilings, and tooled millwork, the room seated the family and servants in comfort. A few weeks before the 1893 holiday, Earl, our butler, and Cook came to me.

"Missy Lura, what should we do? Will we celebrate Thanksgiving this year?"

"What do you mean?"

"Every year, your mother helps Cook plan the menu and oversees the preparation of the manor. Now she sits in her room and takes no interest in our efforts. We are worried."

Struggling with my grief, I turned to Walter for help.

"We have much for which to be thankful. George enjoyed a great life with people who loved him always at his side. You know how happy he was for us and how he was looking forward to the birth of his first grandchild."

"Yes, but what about Thanksgiving?"

"George would want us to celebrate and give thanks for the love that exists in this house. The servants were as much his family as anyone. We owe it to them and your father to go ahead with dinner."

Filling in for Mother, I explained to Earl and Cook that we would proceed with the dinner. "Thanksgiving will be a celebration of Father's life and the love he had for all of us."

As preparations progressed, Mother seemed to be emerging from her depression. She even came down from her suite and helped Cook with the menu. She asked Earl to help with the decorations. He was delighted. Soon the sound of turkeys could be heard coming from the coops, pumpkins were readied for pies, and Thanksgiving decorations adorned the manor. At her insistence, we invited the current staff and all the former servants and their families as well. The size of the guest list swelled to over thirty. Fortunately, the dining room was large enough for two banquet tables and a smaller table for the children. My father had had two fancy claw-foot tables made to his specifications in Boston, each constructed from quartersawn oak with skirted leaves. Without leaves, they were fifty-four inches in diameter. One he kept in the breakfast nook, the other with four leaves was in the dining room. On occasions, such as Thanksgiving and Christmas, where we expected large numbers of guests, both tables were set up in the dining room with all the leaves. Each table could accommodate sixteen people.

A few days before the holiday, Mother pulled Walter aside. "Our tradition has been that George and Earl each deliver a toast. You're now the head of this family. It will be your duty to offer a toast."

Thanksgiving Day, the first heavy storm of the year swept in from the north, leaving behind a foot of snow as it passed through Fairfield County. For the first time in weeks, Mother came down to breakfast full of good cheer. I hugged her. "Mother, you look radiant."

"I am, dear. Thanksgiving was Father's favorite holiday. I intend to enjoy it to the fullest."

"Mother, what is that fragrance? It's so lovely and seems familiar, yet I can't place it."

Mother smiled and closed her eyes. "It's English Fern. Father brought it back from his last trip to England." Before I could comment further, she turned to Walter. "Walter dearest, I have a favor to ask."

"What can I do?"

"This storm has turned Ridgefield into a scene

beautiful enough for a painting, but travel for our guests may be difficult. Would you mind helping with the sleigh? It would be such a relief for me knowing that you will get everyone here."

"Why, that's a wonderful idea." Turning to me, he said, "Lura, you should ride with me when I pick up the last group."

I thought it a lovely idea but worried about Mother.

"Don't fret, Lura, we have plenty of help. I remember my first sleigh ride with your father. He was so nervous, as was I. It was the second time we were alone."

THE DINNER WAS LOVELY. THE AROMA OF COOK'S turkey, along with that of the mincemeat and pumpkin pies, filled the manor.

"Walter, I never realized how many people worked for my parents over the years. It's a good thing Father designed the dining room for large parties."

"Yes, dear. It is a wonderful room and a magnificent party. I haven't seen your mother this happy since George passed."

Earl, as was tradition, gave the first toast thanking the family for our many years of love and support. He ended with tear-filled eyes as he raised his glass, "Mister George—" He could not finish. I rushed to him and held him close.

Walter stood and said, "Thank you, Earl. We all loved Mister George." After a pause, he took his glass in hand. Raising it, he turned, pointing at all the guests and stopped, facing Mother. "Elizabeth Grisham, on behalf of Lura and me and everyone here today, we share in your grief at the loss of George, whom we will never forget. We loved him, and we love you. God bless you both."

Dinner finished, Mother beckoned for Walter. "I'm going to sit in Father's chair in the great room. I would like you to give me five minutes and then bring Lura and all our guests to me."

The room was truly great. The enormous stone fireplace, enclosing a roaring fire, was large enough for a tall man to stand inside with arms straight out to his sides. Chairs and settees enough for all the adults were scattered about. Once we all found a place to sit, with the children on rugs in front of the fire, Walter and I on the piano stool, Mother raised her hands signaling for quiet.

"Thank you all for being here and sharing this wonderful day of thanksgiving with Lura, Walter, and me. Mister George would have loved this."

Many of our guests had tears in their eyes as they listened to Mother's heartfelt words. For several minutes, she let them chat amongst themselves about Mister George and how he was missed. Finally, she raised her hands. The room fell silent. "I've known most of you your entire lives. Your love and devotion has been a godsend, not just since Father went to his

Maker, but for as long as I can recall. I want you to remember this Thanksgiving. Mister George and I had decided on a special gift for each of you this Christmas. I don't want to wait."

A murmur went around the room. Gifts from Mister George and Mother were commonplace. They never forgot a birthday, anniversary, or any other important date. But Christmas in November was not expected. Mother picked up a small basket and set it in her lap. "We have envelopes for all of you. Each contains a Hartford National Bank and Trust draft payable on demand. Mr. Rogers expects to see you all over the next week. Take him the draft, and he will redeem it. For the children, there are banknotes.

AFTER WALTER TOOK OUR GUESTS HOME, AND THE servants had retired, we sat with Mother. She seemed excited and happy. "It was such a wonderful party. Father would have been pleased." She smiled before continuing. "It has been a lovely day and a fine dinner. I'm sure Father was with us in spirit. I felt his presence throughout the day. We will be together again soon."

Although there was a warm fire, I felt a sudden chill. "Mother, don't talk that way. You have many more years to enjoy with us and your grandchildren."

"Why Lura, you talk as if you will have a houseful of children. You might want to talk to Walter."

"Mother, you embarrass me."

"One of our regrets was that you never had brothers or sisters. We built this home with that in mind." After a sip of hot cider, she said, "It's time for me to go, children. Lura, please help me upstairs."

"Walter, I'll be with Mother for a few minutes, please wait for me. We can talk later."

He looked tired but said, "I'll be here if you wish, my darling."

As we entered her suite, tears filled her eyes, and she seemed to slump. "Mother, what's wrong? Are you alright?"

"Yes." Smiling, she embraced me and held me in her arms for the longest time. The slightest hint of English Fern lingered. When she pulled away, she said, "Ah, I have a gift for you."

"What's that?"

Mother sat at her dressing table. She picked up a small, worn box covered in faded red velvet and held it to her bosom. I knew what it contained. Father had given my mother a necklace as a wedding present; it was her most prized possession. Father paid the renowned jeweler, Samuel Ward Benedict, twenty-five-thousand dollars to create a Black Opal pendant. The large center stone came from Australia. At first set in gold with twenty flawless diamonds mounted in an oval around it, the stone's effect was diminished. Mr. Benedict redid the setting in platinum, which set off the opal to a much higher degree. Mother opened the box and gazed upon the cherished jewel. Letting out a sigh, she took it from the box. She stared at it for a long moment and then held it to her heart. As she did, she looked at me with eyes that sparkled with joy.

"Mother, you can't, you must not. I will not allow you."

Holding the pendant in her left hand, she opened her arms wide, "Come, Lura, come."

I knelt as best as my pregnancy would allow. She clasped her arms around me. I didn't know whether to be happy or sad, cry, or laugh. Not knowing what to say, I felt anxiety as my heart alternated between heavy and light. I feared that she was saying goodbye.

"Darling, Father gave me this on our wedding day. I give it to you with the hope that someday you will give it to a daughter of your own. Please don't cry. I want you to have all the happiness that Father's gift brought me." Mother pushed me back on my heels as she put the chain over my head.

"I will cherish this until the day I die." I bent into her arms and kissed her before pressing my face to her bosom.

"Knowing you and Walter will have a wonderful life fills me with joy. I can leave this life happy." Smiling, Mother takes my hands in hers, "I'm ready to join your father, my love."

"Mother, you frighten me. Please don't talk this way."

"Don't be frightened, darling. Now, you must go."

There is a look of serenity, the peacefulness on

her face pushing against the fear building in my chest.

"Is there anything you need?"

"Nothing, but if you and Walter come to my room in a half hour, I would love to have you join me in my evening prayers."

"Nothing would please us more."

Returning to Walter, I cannot avoid a renewed sense of dread. "Mother is acting strangely. She speaks of joining Father."

"She suffers from loneliness without George. I'm of a mind that the celebration has tired her. Once she's had a good night's sleep, she'll be rested, and back to her old self. You'll see." Walter's attempt to reduce my anxiety fails.

Tap, tap. I knock at the door to Mother's room. Not a second passes. "Come, children."

Mother is in bed with the bedclothes pulled to her bosom. A single candle lights the room. She's holding the family Bible to her chest.

"I have two readings to share with you before we pray," she begins. "Darlings, this is from Proverbs 18:22. 'Whoso findeth a wife findeth a good thing, and obtaineth favor of the Lord.'" Finishing, Mother smiles. "You've found one another and bring delight to the Lord and your father and to me. Always remember your love and our love for you."

"My love for Lura is a wonderful thing. I shall cherish her each day for as long as I live."

I can't help myself—tears cover my cheeks as I hold tight to Walter. He bends forward, kissing

Mother. Bending has become more difficult for me as the baby grows inside my ever-expanding stomach. I take Mother's hand and kiss it. She smiles with understanding.

"Let me continue," Mother says. "This is from First Corinthians. 'And unto the married I command, let not the wife depart from her husband.'"

I have a premonition and see Walter shares my concern. Before I can say a word, Mother speaks. "Join me in prayer."

Sitting on the settee near her bed, we clasp our hands in prayer as Mother begins.

"Our father, our one true God, we pray that by your light we are able to dispel the darkness in our hearts." Her prayer complete, she says, "Now, let me rest. I love you both." Walter reaches to put out the candle, but she tells him to leave it.

As we prepare for bed, I experience alarm so strong I ask, "Do you feel this wretchedness that overcomes my heart?"

"No, darling. If your question is about Mother, she seems more at peace than since George's funeral."

I would have said more, but the baby kicked. It isn't the first time, but it caught me by surprise. Putting my hand to my turkey-size stomach, it's there again—stronger. All thoughts of Mother fly from my mind.

"Walter, the baby."

Walter regards me with concern, but as he looks

into my face, he sees nothing is wrong—quite the opposite, something wondrous.

"The baby's kicking. Here, put your hand on my stomach. Do you feel it?"

Walter's face erupts in joy.

IN THE STILL HOURS BEFORE DAWN, I WAKE WITH A chill unlike anything I can remember. Walter appears unaware of the cold as he sleeps with the blanket down to his waist. Not wanting to wake him, I slip from out bed and walk to the window. Despite the chill I felt, the room is quite warm. Outside the snow lies several feet deep for as far as the eye can see. Everything appears normal, but what had caused me such a chill gnawed at my mind. Pulling my nightgown closed. I slip out onto the veranda. As a child, I had loved the strong nature of winter on a quiet winter night or morning, the way I could almost touch the clear, clean, crisp air as it wrapped me in an invisible cloak of exhilaration. It made me feel alive. This is different—the cold, oppressive, weighs me down with fright.

Returning to bed, despite pulling warm covers to my neck, I shiver violently enough to disturb Walter.

"Lura, are you alright?"

I'm not. Mumbling something. I pull Walter's arm around me and pretend to sleep.

The following morning my world, yet again, is forever changed.

FOUR

I WAKE TO SILENCE. WALTER SLEEPS PEACEFULLY AT my side. The baby is no longer kicking. I listen; there's no sound. My heart beats wildly, trying to tear an opening in my chest as if to escape. I recall the premonition of the night before, and once again, dread fills my heart.

"Walter, Walter, wake up."

Walter comes from a deep sleep rubbing his eyes, "What is it? The baby?" He smiles until he sees my face. "Oh, God. What's wrong?"

"It's Mother. I'm so frightened. We must see to her."

Pausing to pull on our robes, we hurry to Mother's rooms. Walter knocks at the door to the suite. No answer. I open the door. With increasing fright, we cross to Mother's bedroom door. I knock.

"Mother? Mother, are you awake?"

Unwilling to wait for an answer, I open the door and step into the even darker room. Walter lights a lamp and walks to her bedside. Mother is unmoving. On her chest rests the family Bible along with an envelope. We can't rouse her.

I put my right hand to her left cheek. There is no warmth. I know, even as I say, "Mother, Mother, please wake up."

"She's gone, my darling, she's gone. There's nothing we can do." Walter takes me in his arms. He pulls me away and helps me to mother's settee.

"Please open the curtains," I say, once I'm sure I will not pass out. He does so.

We sit in silence, unsure what to say for what seems like a lifetime. In truth, it's mere moments before Walter takes charge.

"Lura, we need to clean and dress. Come with me."

"Please, you go. I'll join you in a few minutes. I wish to be with Mother before we begin this new trial."

Walter understands and leaves me. I sense more than see Mother's pendant in my hands.

The few minutes I spend alone with Mother are difficult. I don't cry because I'm angry, angry with Mother.

"How could you do this to me?" I shake my fist at her serene body. "You know how I love you. How can you leave me now? I need you so." I say more unkind things and regret them immediately.

As I sob, I sense Mother's presence. It's as if she's holding me in her arms. I don't hear, but feel her message. "It will be better, child. I'm with Father now, and we're happy."

Wanting to pray, I reach for Mother's Bible and remember the envelope. I'm not sure I want to open it and read her final thoughts alone. I call for the maid and have her fetch Walter.

When he joins me, he tells me to open it. After I read it, I tell Walter she loved him like a son. She wanted us to know that she does not want us to mourn her; she has left—happily—to join Father.

CHRISTMAS COMES WITH A FLURRY OF STORMS. WITH both Father and Mother gone, the house seems empty. We celebrate as best we can, but it is difficult. Walter's parents died years before I met him, and now with Father and Mother gone, we are alone.

The baby kicks more each day. Walter and I discuss redoing the nursery, not knowing if we'll have a boy or girl. Walter hopes it will be a boy. We compromise and leave the walls as they are, for now. Unable to decide where to place the baby's cradle, we leave it along the wall away from the window.

The doctor had assured us the baby would arrive during the last week of January. By afternoon, I am faint and feverish.

Walter brings the doctor to the house who, after he examines me, says, "Neither you nor the baby is in danger, but you should consider traveling to New York where you can receive the best care possible."

"Doctor, what are you saying? Is something wrong with me or the baby?" Terrified, I wrap my arms and shaking hands around my stomach as if shielding our unborn child from harm.

"No. That isn't what I'm saying. You and Walter have been through trying times. You're on the verge of exhaustion. It would be better for you and the baby if you had specialized care."

Walter and I exchange glances, and I can see the concern in his face. "Tell us what we should do."

The doctor pulls his spectacles off and cleans them on his coat. I've seen him do this many times over the years. He wants time to think before he speaks. Letting out a sigh, he answers Walter's question.

"Lura and the baby are fine, but I don't want to take any chances. There's a doctor in New York who specializes in caring for women with child. He can give you much better care than I can. Besides, there's a hospital with a children's ward, New York Hospital, where you can go when it's time for the birth. The doctors and nurses can give you twenty-four-hour care before, during, and after the birth of your child."

Walter looks at me with a plea that I can almost hear. "We've lost Father and Mother."

"I know. We can't take the chance. We'll leave as soon as we can travel," I say in answer to his unspoken question.

Turning to the doctor, I ask, "Can you make the

arrangements in New York for us? You can let them know we will be taking a suite at the Waldorf Hotel."

"I'll send a telegraph today. I should have an answer no later than tomorrow afternoon."

We thank the doctor and Walter walks him to the door. Thinking I can't hear them, Walter asks, "Are you sure Lura and the baby are fine?"

"Yes. Lura's exhausted, and she refuses to stay in bed. Get her to New York, and the doctor will provide her with nurses around the clock. They will ensure that she gets the rest she needs. Promise me, you will both get some rest."

"I'm not tired, Doctor."

"Walter, you're physically fine. It's another condition that requires rest. It has to do with mental exhaustion. The term to describe the diagnosis—stress—is relatively new. We know little about it, but we know the cure includes rest."

"I have a railroad to run. I can't stop working."

"You could turn some of the responsibility and day-to-day tasks over to your staff, as much for Lura's sake as yours. She can't suffer another loss."

While I didn't know it at the time, Walter took the doctor's advice and turned much of the operation of the railroad over to his trusted assistant. He relinquished control much the same as Father had done when Walter and I had married. He made it possible for Father to enjoy his retirement, short-lived as it was.

Walter and I hold each other for a long minute

when he rejoins me. Not wanting him to know how worried I am, I make light of the trip. "The Waldorf Hotel is the newest and without a doubt one of the most luxurious hotels in the world. Did you know it was finished?"

"No. I didn't." Walter goes along with the charade that we're going on a holiday.

"Well, you should have. I read it in *The Evening Telegram*. It's on the corner of Fifth Avenue and Thirty-Third Street. William Waldorf Astor tore down the family mansion and built the largest hotel in the world."

"Do tell." Walter's smiling.

"Don't tease. The hotel was completed earlier this year, and I expect you to book us a suite. I don't care what it costs or what you must do to get it. If you can't, I will."

"What do you mean if I can't, you will?"

I can't tell if he's surprised or annoyed.

"Father once had to deal with those nasty people at Tammany Hall to get a spur approved. Thomas Gilroy, the Commissioner of Public Works and a powerbroker at Tammany Hall, and Father became friends, though I'll never understand what Father saw in that man."

"Darling, will you please get to the point?"

"Mr. Gilroy is now Mayor Gilroy. I'm sure he can get us into the Waldorf."

We didn't need to resort to asking Mayor Gilroy for help. Mr. Astor was acquainted with the Grisham

Railroad and was more than happy to accommodate us. Little did he or I anticipate the length of my stay.

FIVE

I'M JOSEPH MYER, WALTER'S HALF-BROTHER. I doubt he knows I exist. Until shortly before Mother died, I believed my father had died in the Civil War, not long before I was born. I was always proud that he had served but not pleased that he hadn't married my mother; God rest her soul.

Mother passed away two years ago. It's time I introduce myself to Walter. Our father loved both our mothers. Of that, I'm certain. Had he known of my existence, I'm sure he would have shown me the same love he bestowed upon Walter.

Mother served as a nurse in the Union Army. What made it unusual was that she was born and raised in Tennessee, a Confederate state. She suffered after the war because of both. Shunned by the Union carpetbaggers who had no mercy for Tennesseans, and the townspeople where she raised me knew

Mother had served in the Union Army. They considered her a traitor and treated us as badly as they did the freed slaves. It helped me grow strong and become a fighter. I fought almost every day until I went north to college in New York.

"Joseph, you must have an education if you're to succeed in this world. Here in the south, you will be denied your right to that. In New York, you will have the same opportunity as every other student, regardless of your birth."

I argued with her. I didn't want to leave, nor did I want the money she had saved and gone without for twenty years so I could have an education.

"Mother, I can't."

"You must. Do it for me."

In the end, she won out, and I made my way to New York. With her money, my winnings from prizefighting, and scholarships, I managed to graduate from Columbia College and was accepted to Columbia Law School. For the son of a Union sympathizer, there was no chance of success in Tennessee. I stayed in New York, hung out my shingle, and built a successful practice.

Not long after I started my law practice, I needed the services of private detectives. After several bad experiences with locals, I began a search for competent investigators. Over lunch with my friend, Louis Brandeis, I broached the subject.

"Louis, I must thank you for introducing me to Delmonico's. It is, without a doubt, the finest restaurant in New York."

"It's the only one in the country with a world-wide reputation. But, I sense that you have something else on your mind." Sparing us additional chitchat, he added, "Is it something I can help you with?"

"I could use your advice, but it's too trivial to bother you with."

"Go ahead, but you've never taken my advice before."

"'If you mean when you tell me, 'Joseph why must you insist on wearing the old bowler and that ugly black topcoat?' I'll remind you my mother gave me the bowler, and the topcoat reminds me of my first successful trial.'"

"You'll never learn."

"I've found myself in need of a good private detective. The ones that I've used have been sorely lacking. I wonder if you might have one or two you could recommend."

"No problem. I've got the perfect recommendation. Have you ever heard of the Pinkerton Detective Agency?"

"The name is familiar. Go on."

"They've been in business since 1850 and have the highest standards. I've never been disappointed in their work. I'll put you in touch with Donald White. He heads up their New York office."

I met with Mr. White a few days later. He explained that while the Pinkertons would always do its best to satisfy my investigative needs, I needed to understand that the results might not always be what I want or expect.

"Thank you, Mr. White. I appreciate your honesty. That said, I would like to hire your agency to handle a personal matter."

The detective he assigned to my family search established that my father had died as a result of his lingering war wounds. At least that part of what my mother had told me about him was true. What she left out was he had died three years after the war.

White told me my father had one other child, a son. "Your half-brother, Walter, was an engineer for Grisham Railroad, now he owns it. He married the owner's daughter. When his father-in-law, George Grisham, died, he took control. His mother-in-law has since passed away."

"What else can you tell me about him?"

"Mrs. Myer is expecting. Her doctor wants her to come to New York to see doctors who specialize in caring for women with child."

"When they arrive in New York, alert me and tell me where they are staying."

SIX

NEW YEAR'S EVE, DECEMBER 31, 1893, IS SPECTAC-
ular. The Waldorf hosts a magnificent ball for its
guests. The gown I wear does little to conceal the fact
that I'm with child. If it weren't for the opportunity
to meet Mr. Astor, I would have remained in our
suite.

The concierge introduces us to Mr. Astor, who
has traveled from his home in England for the gala.

"Mr. Myer, Mrs. Myer, it's an honor to meet you.
Your father and I were partners in several business
projects before I gave up my law practice and moved
to England. A frank and honorable man, I developed
a warm appreciation of him. I was saddened to learn
of his passing."

"Thank you, Mr. Astor. Father often spoke of
you and the trust he placed in you. That's the reason
Walter and I chose the Waldorf." I stepped forward

and kissed Mr. Astor on the cheeks in the European manner. "Why, Mr. Astor, I believe I've embarrassed you. If so, please accept my humblest apologies."

"No, madam. I'm flattered that you would bestow your kisses upon a man of my advanced age." He's forty-five and an attractive man.

Standing next to me, Walter enjoys every word of our conversation. Excusing myself, I leave the two men and return to our suite; dressing for the gala, and visiting with acquaintances, has taken its toll. Besides, in my present condition, I'm far from attractive. I'm what the good doctor wanted me to avoid—exhausted.

Walter, always the dear, comes to our suite once he says goodnight to our host. Mr. Astor, the father of five children himself, understood my condition and Walter's concern.

Waiting for the New Year to arrive, we step out on the balcony. Fifth Avenue is alive with people and carriages of every description. Even though the temperature can't be more than twenty-five degrees, and there's a light snow falling, nothing seems to dampen the celebrants' spirits.

As we reflect on the year's end, Walter takes me into his arms. "My marriage to you has been the happiest experience of my life. Nothing will ever equal the joy I felt when Pastor Carter pronounced us man and wife."

I kiss Walter and tease him. "Won't the birth of our child be the happiest moment in your life?"

"It will be. But it will be happiness of a different nature. Now let's get inside before you, and he, freeze to death."

Once in bed, I think of the loss of my father and mother. "Only you and I remain of our families. We're as alone as orphans."

"No, that's not true. We have one another and will soon have a child. We were blessed to be loved by George and Elizabeth. We will be blessed again when Little George is born."

Before I can answer, the bells of the city begin to ring in the New Year. We rush to the window and enjoy the spectacular fireworks display.

WE WAKE TO A FRESH STORM THAT COVERS THE CITY in a blanket of icy snow. The nurse that the doctor had insisted upon arrives with the boy delivering our morning coffee.

"Nurse, you can take the day off. Go home and enjoy your family. I can take care of Mrs. Myer for one day."

"But Mr. Myer, I'm responsible for the mistress and the care of your unborn child. The doctor will be angry with me if I leave her without proper care."

"Be off with you. If the doctor becomes angry, he can be annoyed with me. Now go home." Walter smiles, gathers up the nurse's belongings, drapes her cloak over her shoulders, walks her to the door, and pushes her out.

We talk about our future and our child. For the life of me, Walter remains positive we'll have a boy. He continues to insist, "The boy will be like your father. That's why we shall name him George Walter Myer."

"If that's what you want. It seems as I have no choice but to bow to your will." I become serious. "Tomorrow, we must visit the doctor and the hospital. Why does he insist that I deliver the child there? You and I, and our parents before us, were all born at home."

"Lura, we've talked about this many times. The doctor insists that the birth will be much safer at the hospital under his care and with trained nurses in attendance."

"But the papers tell of people who go to hospitals only to contract some malady or other. Hospitals are where people die. I don't want to die in a hospital."

"You will not. I promise."

Walter makes a New Year's prediction. "Eighteen ninety-four will be the happiest year of your life."

Like the night Mother died, I wake with a sense of peril. The time is 4:00 a.m. Walter sleeps soundly at my side

Death is in the cold, still air.

SEVEN

JANUARY 2, 1894: DAWN IS INVISIBLE IN THE GRAY and sleet-filled sky. It doesn't abate with the fog obscuring the sun. Upset from the early morning premonition, I must get outside and experience the winter air. Walter agrees to a short walk; it will allow him to finish his cigar.

Cold has many faces. Safe at home, cold is clear with sparkling, crisp air as it surrounds one in an invisible coat of exhilaration. With the stunning winter surrounding, one can almost feel the vivid blue of the sky that brings my soul to life, even at zero degrees. I love the wonder of it all. Manhattan is the opposite. The cold close—oppressive—smothers us in a dreary, hideous world in which every other living soul and I become depressed. The cold bores into my soul, chilling hope.

"Walter, please take me back to the hotel."

WALTER WANTS TO RESCHEDULE OUR APPOINTMENT with the doctor.

"There isn't enough time for a messenger to reach the doctor. We don't have to leave here until ten. I'm sure the weather will clear by then."

Walter agrees to my insistence on visiting the doctor regardless of the weather. I should have listened to him. It's a decision I will regret to my dying day.

From our twelfth-floor suite, I have an unobstructed view of Fifth Avenue. The sleet has not let up. It's difficult to see clearly, but a few people walk the avenue, hunched over and moving slowly. The cabs are doing a brisk business. Pedestrians are dressed for the rain and sleet, as are the cab drivers, with slickers over heavy woolen coats. I see cabs rushing as they sweep in and around other hacks and delivery wagons. Near collisions abound.

Walter's hesitant to expose me to the weather and pleads, "It's not safe. We can see the doctor another time."

"Will you please call for a cab?" I don't heed his arguments.

He concedes and rings for a bellman. "Please have a cab available for us in thirty minutes."

When we exit the Waldorf, the weather has worsened, and I'm tempted to return to our suite. Walter's right. We can go another day, but I've spent considerable time preparing for this difficult trip and must be sure the baby isn't in danger. The cab is

THE MONA LISA SISTERS

standing by for us. I look at Walter, whose eyes plead
with me to reconsider.

"Let's be about our business. The doctor is
expecting us."

The short walk from the hotel lobby to the cab
is an ordeal. A doorman and Walter help me, each
with a firm grip on an arm; a second doorman holds
an umbrella above us. It blows away before we reach
the Hansom cab. I have difficulty getting into the
swaying vehicle. The horse stamps its feet as the
driver does his best to keep his body protected by the
back of the cab as he hunches over in the cold and
rain. It must be terrible for him as he holds the reins
and whip in one hand while pulling down his top hat
with the other. How can he see?

I should have listened to Walter.

EIGHT

SEAN O'BANNON IS TIRED, AND HE'S DRUNK.
Second-generation Irish, he can't read or write, but
he knows his numbers. Because of this, he was able
to secure work delivering beer. His day starts at four
in the morning, and by eight, he's usually drunk.
Today's no exception. An empty one replaces each
barrel he delivers; they are rarely completely dry. By
tipping them on end, he gets a half-pint of tepid beer,
sometimes more. The delivery wagon, pulled by two
horses, holds forty barrels. He has two more
deliveries before he can go home to his nagging wife
and the five little ones.

The icy slush on the road makes it hard to
control the team and keep the wagon from slipping,
especially for a drunk. The sleet doesn't make things
any easier. O'Bannon is in a hurry to finish his
deliveries so he can pass out in his warm bed. He uses

the whip viciously. Already on edge, the startled team breaks into a run. Falling back, he loses the reins. The horses are out of control, running and slipping on the slick and mushy roadway. O'Bannon reaches down and tries to grab the reins as the team careens into a cab.

O'Bannon will not have to worry about explaining the accident to his boss. He's dead from a broken neck.

Sadly, he isn't the only one to die.

NINE

As we start our journey, the wind increases, causing the cab to teeter from side to side. I'm frightened, and I can see that Walter's upset. I want his forgiveness, but before I can speak, I'm slammed against the door. There's a tremendous sound, and the cab is on its side. A horse's scream fills the air and then all is still as my world turns dark.

As the cab rolls over, I'm thrown out. I find myself face down in the cold muck. Before I pass out, I sense, more than taste, dirty, slushy snow, salt, soot, urine, and something I can't quite place. Regaining consciousness, I wipe horse dung from my face and coat. My clothes are saturated with beer.

Now I'm bouncing and slipping. I hurt everywhere. Where am I? Sounds cut through the darkness. My head hurts; my stomach is a searing pain. Where am I? Dear Lord. The baby, Walter. Opening my eyes, I see a strange man bent over me. He's holding me. "Where am I? Who are you?"

"You're in an ambulance. We're taking you to New York Hospital."

"Please slow down. My baby, you're hurting the baby." I have a contraction.

The attendant tells me not to worry. "We'll have you at the hospital in a few minutes."

"Where is my husband?"

"I don't know."

"What happened?"

He stops speaking and glances out a grimy window. The ambulance is a horrible wooden thing with benches on both sides. There are dark red stains on the walls; there are even some on the roof over my head. They must be bloodstains. I'm on one side, the attendant on the other. The walls are a horrid gray—they match the weather—the windows covered with soot. Hell must look like this.

"We're at the hospital. Please lie back. We'll carry you in on the stretcher."

I have a contraction. It's too soon. Carried into the hospital, I silently pray. *Dear Lord, please let the baby live.* The next hours are a combination of contractions, worry, and ever-increasing pain.

"Where is my husband? I need my husband."

My pleas meet with, "I don't know. We're trying to save the baby."

"Ma'am, we need to put you to sleep now. Please

breathe deeply." A nurse bends over me and puts a black rubber device over my mouth and nose. I fight at first, but the more I breathe the sweet-smelling vapors, the less I struggle—then oblivion.

When I open my eyes, I'm in a room surrounded by beds. It looks like what military barracks must be. A long hall, there must be at least a dozen cots lining each wall. On each rests a woman, half of whom are moaning. The odor of vomit, urine, and feces is appalling. It isn't much different than the foul stench in the ambulance. Where am I? Where's Walter? The baby? My hands fly to my stomach. It's flat. I realize that I've had the baby.

Where is my baby? Looking around, I see there are no nurses. Trying to rise, I find I cannot. I have no strength. I call for a nurse.

"It's no use, dearie. They only come 'round on the half hour," the woman to my right says.

"What is this place?"

"The charity ward. Poor folk don't rate a full-time nurse. Only rich people get that."

It's hours before a nurse comes through the ward, accompanied by a pair of female attendants who clean and change the bedpans. Her attitude toward the patients, including me, is curt.

"Nurse, I need your attention," I call to her, but she acts as though she doesn't hear me. It takes all my strength to call out again. Still, she ignores my pleas.

My anger is a lump of red-hot coal. I don't know where it comes from, but I yell loud enough to draw the attention of not only the nurse but everyone on the floor as the room goes silent.

I tell her who my doctor is and demand to see him. She recognizes his name and understands that I must not be a charity case.

Within minutes, another nurse and two attendants appear at my bedside. I'm fawned over and transferred to a rolling gurney. In the blink of an eye, I'm in a private room with a fulltime nurse. One of the hospital's doctors, Dr. Samuels, arrives full of apologies and excuses. Aside from the apologies, I can tell something is amiss. I haven't seen Walter or the baby.

"Where is my husband? My child?"

Dr. Samuels says, "Please, give me a few minutes." And with that, he turns and hurries from the room. When he returns, an older man dressed in black with a clerical collar is with him. The significance of the man's dress isn't lost on me.

My world begins to collapse. It can't be. I will not, I cannot, believe it.

"Mrs. Myer, this is the Reverend Davis. He's the hospital chaplain."

"I demand to see my husband and child. Where are they?"

The chaplain comes to the side of my bed and reaches for my hand. I pull it back. I don't want any connection to this man.

"Mrs. Myer, I have sad news. Your husband died in the accident."

My heart, my entire being, my soul, seem to collapse. I gasp for breath; I can't swallow. This is a mistake—it must be someone else's husband.

"Do you wish me to pray with you?"

"Pray? Do you think I want to pray? You just told me my husband's dead." The man I wanted to spend the rest of my life with is dead, and this foolish man wants me to pray. I wish I were dead. I gaze at him and shake my head from side to side.

"My child, where is my child?"

"You haven't told her?" The chaplain turns a surprised face towards Dr. Samuels.

The doctor looks like he would rather answer any question but mine. Once again, I sense by their discomfort what's coming. My child is gone—I want him to say it. Our gazes lock.

"Go ahead, Doctor, tell me where my child is."

"As you know, Mrs. Myer, you were in a serious accident. The injuries you suffered caused you to go into labor."

"Where is my child?"

"I'm sorry. We did all we could, but by the time we delivered him, he'd died of his injuries."

"I demand to see my child."

"I don't think that would be a good idea."

"And why is that, Doctor?"

"You are a gentlewoman, much too delicate."

"While you may think I'm too delicate, let me tell you, if you don't bring my child to me, you will answer with your job. Do I make myself clear, Doctor?"

"Yes."

George Walter Grisham is beautiful. I hold his still body in my arms; curly dark brown hair covers his tiny head. He would have been everything Walter and I had dreamed of in our child. The tears shock had robbed me of begin to flow until great racking sobs torment me, and I rage against the cruel fate that has taken everything from me: my parents, my husband, and my son.

A week later, the doctor releases me from New York Hospital. In my mind, it will always remain a place where people die. Returning to the Waldorf, they have kept the suite for me that I had shared with Walter. I can't lie in the same bed where we last slept. Taking another suite, I remain no longer than required. As soon as I'm well enough to travel, I take my son and husband home to Grisham Manor.

I bury them next to Father and Mother.

TEN

I MOURNED SO THAT I THOUGHT I, TOO, SHOULD die. I became a recluse and refused to face the grief that consumed me. The reality of my life became so dark and horrific, I permitted it to lock me away in Grisham Manor.

When Father died, Emily had obtained several bolts of Courtauld's black crape anglais for Mother's mourning dresses. Enough remained for me to have several dresses made. All were the same dull black floor-to-neck garment. I didn't allow any frill or lace. They served as symbols—daily reminders—of the loss of my loved ones, Father, Mother, Walter, and Little George. They became the chains that bound me to my self-made prison.

"Each is to be identical. You will begin with a buttoned neck and end with an unadorned floor-length skirt. The sleeves will be straight and fit tightly around my wrists." It wasn't until months later that I finally appreciated how ugly they were.

My anger and depression impacted—harmed—the household staff. It's a wonder they didn't abandon me.

The only time I leave the house is to visit the family graves. The clear, crisp cold I so loved no longer holds any beauty for me. The life I enjoyed in the Connecticut winter months is nowhere to be found. The snow is something to be cleared from the graves. I lack the strength or will to sweep it away. Earl handles that chore, early each morning, before I make my daily visit.

My dearest friend, Emily Bartolini, came daily only to be turned away by Earl with a formal, "Mrs. Myer isn't seeing guests today." Earl knew how close Emily and I were. He had been our butler for thirty years and had, in ways, become like an uncle to me. A lifelong bachelor, he cared deeply for the family, especially me. A few months after I returned from New York, he visited Emily's home.

Emily and I could not have been more different. Maybe that was why we were so close. Her father owned Bartolini's Mercantile. He began there as a stock boy after service in the Civil War. His industrious ways saw him advance through every job within the business; he has owned the store for the last fifteen years. Where I'm tall and slim with a full bosom, Emily is short with almost none. I doubt she stands above five-foot-three. Emily has the same dark Italian features as her father, not to mention she shares his business acumen. On her short frame, she carries my weight and more. Her raven hair cut in the short style coming into vogue, her choice is not fashion-driven. She has always hated spending the hours I do brushing and combing my much longer tresses. I love her as if she were my sister. I doubt we could care as much for each other if we were sisters.

"Miss Emily, please forgive my impertinence, but I must speak with you about Missy Lura."

"Oh, Earl, please come in. I've been so worried."

"Miss Emily, I fear she may die if nothing is done. She sits alone all day in the great room. She stares out the window and speaks naught. Each morning she visits the graves for a few minutes. When she returns to the house, she sits until late afternoon."

"Is that all she's doing, nothing more?"

"In the afternoon, she returns to the graves and sits in silence. Before her visits, I tidy up and clear the graves."

"Is she eating? Does she clean herself?"

"She eats like a mouse, hardly enough to keep her alive. The chambermaid tells me most nights she sleeps in her dress and often refuses to put on a fresh one in the morning. Missy Lura barely allows the woman to brush out and comb her hair."

"Earl, I come almost every day only to be turned away."

"I know."

"What is it you want from me?"

"We must save her. Come today, and I'll not turn you away."

"I'll come, though she may refuse to see me."

"I know, Miss Emily. Nevertheless, I beg you to come. If she refuses to speak with you, at least she'll know you're concerned."

"I'll see you at three. Thank you for coming."

As Earl rises to leave, Emily hugs the old man, and with tears in her eyes, kisses his rough cheek. "Thank you, Earl. Thank you ever so much."

I DON'T CARE IF I LIVE OR DIE.

Days become weeks, and weeks become months as I spend my days sealed in the cage of sorrow. This grief will not bring my family back, but everything depresses me, and the winter is unusually severe. The gloomy gray weather does nothing to improve my spirits. I pray for a miracle while sitting in Father's chair.

"Dear Lord, please help me. My world is dark and gray, full of pain and sadness. I pray you guide me from this. In this, I beseech you. Amen."

Crushed by the enormity of my loss and weak from lack of eating, I cannot sleep. Once I pray, something happens that I haven't experienced in months. I feel as though Walter is near, and I fall asleep.

"Lura . . . Lura." Somewhere in my dream, I hear

a familiar voice. It comes like a welcome break from the horror I've been living.

"Lura, it's me, Walter. Can you hear me?"

"Yes. Where are you? I can't see you."

"Push your fear aside and look for me on the edge of the shadows. I'm here and will be when your need is great."

"Oh, Walter, I miss you so. I miss them, too, but the pain of your loss is the greatest. I want to join you, I want to."

"You mustn't think such a thought. You have much to live for."

"My life is nothing but days of unending sadness and pain."

"There is a way out. You must escape the chains that threaten to destroy you and embrace the love you're capable of sharing."

"I shared my love with you, and now you are gone."

"I'll never be completely gone, never as long as you keep a piece of our love in your heart. But you must live, you have to live, for our son and me."

"Oh, Walter, how can I?"

"By opening your heart to love. It's my wish that—"

"Walter."

"Lura, wake up. Please, you're dreaming."

Opening my eyes, Walter's gone, but my dearest friend, Emily, holds my hands in hers. His visit is a sign that I must try. Emily's presence confirms it.

"Oh, Lura, I've missed you so. Please don't send me away."

"Emily . . . oh, I've missed you so."

I haven't cried since Walter died. I sob as Emily takes me in her arms. Soon we're both in tears. Earl must have heard us because he comes into the room. I give him what must be a strange-looking smile. He has tears streaming down his cheeks, but he's smiling. What is this? He gives a small bow and backs out, slowly closing the door.

Things will be better. Thank you, Lord, a silent prayer. I know I'll recover.

After what seems an eternity, Emily and I are cried out. Exhausted, we can barely speak. Earl must have been at the door waiting because, within a minute, he appears with steaming mugs of hot cocoa and fresh-baked molasses cookies. My emotions are beyond control. Coming to my feet, I do something I haven't done in many years—I throw my arms around this man who has always been in my life.

"Oh, Earl. I know you brought Emily. I'm so sorry for the way I've treated you. Can you ever forgive me?"

Earl is the most reserved man I've ever known. He surprises me for the second time this day. After a moment, he hugs me back. He has tears in his eyes.

"I love you, Missy Lura. We have missed you so much." We hold each for a long moment. Then, the old Earl is back. He releases me, wipes his eyes, stands stiffly, and says, "Will that be all, Mrs. Myer?

If so, I will leave you ladies to your refreshment."

Emily and I can't stop talking. Before we realize the time, Earl returns. "Mrs. Myer, Miss Emily, dinner will be served in one hour. If you care to change, I'll send the maid to you."

"EMILY, DO HELP ME OUT OF THIS UGLY WIDOW'S garb and into something more appropriate for having dinner with my best friend. The woman who may have saved my life. Did I tell you that you are the answer to my prayers?"

Wearing a light green spring dress to dinner, I want Earl, the rest of the staff, and maybe myself, to see that I'm going to get better and will mend. In the looks and smiles they share as Emily and I are served, they know I will heal.

Emily promises to return the following morning. I relish a glimmer of happiness for the first time in months.

Before retiring, I pray. "Dear Lord, I thank you for the love you've shown me this day. Thank you for allowing Earl to be in my life. I will never forget what he did, with your guidance, for me. I miss my family sorely, but you will protect and guide me to a life of love. Amen."

It seems as though I'm asleep before I close my eyes. When I rise in the morning, the sun has returned to Grisham Manor. The snowstorms are gone, and spring is upon us. The maid has laid out a colorful dress for me. I smile and ring for her.

"Thank you. This dress is perfect for this wonderful day."

"Will madam wish breakfast in her room?"

"No. Once I visit the family, I'll join Cook in the kitchen for whatever she has prepared."

After I bundle up, I let myself out and visit the family. When I return from the graves, I accept that they're dead and their spirits are with the Lord in heaven, but I feel close to them.

"Dear family, I've been so sad and lonely all these terrible months. Yesterday, God visited me. My life will never be the same without you. I will always love and miss you, but God has shown me that I can live and be happy. Earl brought dear Emily back into my life. I love them both. You will always be in my heart as I begin this part of my life."

Walking back to the house, I know they would understand and approve.

"I must not let you down," I say, looking back at the graves.

"EMILY, I'M NOT READY TO FACE THE TOWNSPEOPLE yet. Please, give me a few more days." I've lost a great deal of weight and feel weak. I doubt any of my dresses will fit.

Emily and Earl seem like conspirators determined to get me to town. "All right, Lura, we will give you until Sunday."

"Sunday?"

They ignore me as Earl says, "Miss Emily, I'll have the carriage at your door bright and early. You will do us the honor of a light repast before I drive you to church. I'll remain with the coachman until the service is over. Does that meet with your approval?"

"Yes, it does. Thank you, Earl. Have you spoken to the pastor?"

"Yes, ma'am. He will ensure that the Grisham pew is ready for you ladies."

I can hardly believe my ears. These two people, whom I love dearly, speak as if I'm a child or not present. "Excuse me, dear friends, but do I not have a say in what I shall do on the Sabbath?"

Earl smiles. Emily looks me in the eye, and with a shake of her head, says, "No, you do not."

"I'll go with you if Earl drives and agrees to sit with us."

Earl, embarrassed, but at the same time pleased, agrees. Pastor Carter has long since accepted Emily into his church, always choosing to ignore the fact that she remains Catholic.

"What had you and Walter decided about your honeymoon? I know he wanted to take you to Paris."

I had not thought about Paris since the day Walter died. "Oh, Emily, I can't imagine such a thing without Walter."

"Walter would want you to move on with your life. He loved Paris. He always spoke of it as the one place in the world that he wanted to take you. Go. Honor his memory."

"How can I leave? There's the manor, the railroad. I have responsibilities."

Emily stares at me, and I swear she's going to scold me, but she laughs.

"How can I go to Paris?"

"You've ignored the manor and the railroad for months. Both are running fine. Earl has run this household for decades, even before you were born. Do you think your mother didn't rely on him and the staff?"

"She did. But what about the railroad?"

"Again, Lura dear, you've ignored it for months. Walter and your father hired the most qualified and honest managers. They have been in charge since the day you and Walter left for New York. They will continue to see to your interests."

"Are you sure I can trust them?"

"Yes, but if you're worried, sell them the railroad."

"What are you saying? Father built it from the ground up. It's part of my life, Father's legacy."

"But how long do you think this world we live in will allow a woman to run such an enterprise? The other railroads will be after you like wolves upon a newborn calf."

"Maybe you're right, but I'm not ready for Paris. Not yet."

ELEVEN

FATHER HAD SEVERAL LAWYERS, ONE FIRM FOR THE railroad, another for his landholdings, and yet another for his overseas investments. These men had been guests in our home many times over the years. However, I wasn't involved in any of the business meetings or transactions. In that regard, they were strangers. I decided to set up a series of meetings with the attorneys, the railroad managers, and Emily's father.

After meeting with the lawyers and the railroad men, I invite Mr. Bartolini to dine with me. I don't invite Emily. After we finish dinner, I ask Mr. Bartolini to join me in Father's study. Bookcases cover one wall, the shelves, from floor to ceiling, are laden with books from throughout the world. This room is where, at my father's knee, I learned French and German. He read in whatever language the work was written. Afterward, he discussed the subject with me in that same language. Behind Father's desk is a large window overlooking the river and the forest beyond. The walls are of dark mahogany. I've always loved this room. Now my study, it has become my haven.

"Please have one," I say, offering Mr. Bartolini father's cigar box.

"No, Mrs. Myer, I can't smoke in the presence of a lady."

"Mr. Bartolini, I've been in your home and store many a time while you enjoyed a good cigar. These are the finest cigars."

"But this is different, Mrs. Myer. I can't—"

"Mr. Bartolini, I've always been Lura to you. I insist that you call me by my given name and that you smoke one of these fine cigars. We can't let them go to waste. Besides, in a very unladylike manner, I shall pour a tumbler of good Tennessee whiskey for each of us. I will countenance no argument."

Before he can object, I select a fine thick cigar and using father's silver cutter, I cut it, light it, and hand it to him. Mr. Bartolini's jaw drops, his eyes open with a look best described as aghast.

"I began cutting and lighting my father's cigars as a child. It might surprise you to know that on occasion, I've smoked one myself."

Once we're settled and taste the whiskey, Mr. Bartolini asks, "And why have you invited me here tonight, dear lady . . . Lura?"

"Father said you're one of the most honest men he ever knew. He confided in me that he tried to hire you away from the mercantile to run the supply organization for the railroad, but that you wished to remain your own man, able to spend every free moment with your family."

"That's true. But what do you need of me?"

"I plan to sell the railroad, most of my property holdings, and consolidate my investments. I want your advice."

"My Lord. I do not know such things. My advice would be of no value to you."

"On the contrary, I've met with father's lawyers regarding these issues. They were father's counselors. They are not mine. I don't know them, nor their attitude toward women, specifically rich widows."

"I don't see how I can help you."

"Regardless of the potential profit to yourself, you will give me honest counsel. I want to hire you to assist me in a search."

"What kind of search?"

"Find the best, the brightest, the most honest attorney you can to advise me in these decisions. I want one in whom I can place complete confidence with the same trust I have for you."

"I'm honored by your request."

"I have the feeling that you have already decided to help me."

"I have, Lura, but there's one condition."

"And what is that, Mr. Bartolini?"

"Please call me Giovanni."

"Thank you, Giovanni. You've removed a great burden from my shoulders."

A MONTH LATER, GIOVANNI SUGGESTS THAT HE and I meet with Mr. Louis Brandeis in his New York branch office. He explained that Mr. Brandeis was in New York so often his firm, Warren and Brandeis, maintained a branch office and an apartment there. When we met, the door was unlocked, and we let ourselves in. I was surprised at the spartan furnishing of the space. There was no receptionist. There were two old rolltop desks; both appeared to be so alike they had to be from the Sears, Roebuck catalog, probably black walnut. It seems one was for his partner, Samuel Warren, and the second was his. A man in shirtsleeves was at the open desk with his back to us. He seemed to be absorbed in his work. Giovanni and I took the two other chairs in the room. After a moment, Giovanni said, "Brandeis."

As the man turned, he muttered a gruff, "What?" and then "Bartolini." He stood, and the two men shook hands.

"Louis, may I introduce Mrs. Walter Myer."

"Mrs. Myer, may I present Mr. Louis Brandeis."

After the introductions, Mr. Brandeis wasted no time in getting down to business.

"Mrs. Myer, I must admit that when Mr.

Bartolini called upon me, I was tempted to dismiss him and your request out of hand. As you know, I sent him packing when he first approached."

"What caused you to rethink your decision?"

"Several things, not the least being Mr. Bartolini's persistence."

"Was my wealth and holdings a factor?"

"Not in the way you might imagine, Mrs. Myer."

"I'm intrigued. Please go on."

"Even though I represented the Wisconsin Central Railroad five years ago, I'm now normally a foe of anything to do with the railroads and the monopolies they foist upon the people. Representing one will be a challenge for me. You should know that before we talk further."

"Mr. Brandeis, you will be representing me, not my railroad. Mr. Bartolini has recommended you as the one attorney who can be counted on to represent all my interests in the manner I desire. No one is to be advantaged or disadvantaged in any transaction. We have conducted inquires, and I agree that you're the one choice. Will you do me the honor of accepting my proposal?"

"Yes, I will. Now we have a few issues to settle."

"I believe those issues easily handled. Here is an initial retainer of twenty-five thousand dollars." When I reach out to him with the draft, Mr. Brandeis hesitates a moment and then takes the envelope. Without opening it, he places inside his desk. "My firm is based in Boston, so I'll be able to visit you and

Giovanni often on my trips back and forth."

"Please draw up an agreement and a Power of Attorney for Mr. Bartolini. He'll be your point of contact. He'll make all decisions on my behalf."

Mr. Bartolini objects. I cut him off and hand him another envelope. "Giovanni, this is a bank draft in the same amount. You will work with Mr. Brandeis and will receive the same compensation as he."

"But Lura, this is more money than I make in five years. I can't accept this."

"You dishonor me if you do not. With this and the money you earn representing me, you will be able to retire and enjoy the rewards you deserve. Don't worry. I believe that what you and Mr. Brandeis do for me will be far more difficult and challenging than you can imagine. Am I right, Mr. Brandeis?"

"Yes, Mrs. Myer. This will be a task of monumental dimensions. Mr. Bartolini will earn every dime he garners."

Addressing Giovanni, he continues, "I've perused the papers you provided me. Even if these were all the holdings, and I'm sure there are more, you and I'll meet with attorneys, managers, and potential buyers for at least two years, quite possibly longer. You should divest yourself of your mercantile."

Mr. Bartolini divests himself of the store by giving it to Emily.

"Emily, you must go with me to Paris. It was your idea, after all."

"I would love to travel to Paris with you, but that's impossible. You're the reason. Once my father accepted your offer and gave me the mercantile, I've had no time for anything but the store."

"Must you blame me for everything?" We cannot help but laugh.

"I may be running away, but you have the opportunity to prove that women can succeed in business. You will have several stores operating by the turn of the century. You will flourish."

"I know, Lura. It's a wonderful opportunity. Father and I both appreciate what you are doing for us."

"Don't look at it that way. Your father and Mr. Brandeis have taken a great load from my shoulders. I can travel without worrying about operating or divesting myself of these holdings. The man I trust most is working with the attorney we trust to protect my holdings and me. They will ensure that I retain my wealth and see to it that it continues to grow."

"Father would die before dishonoring your trust in him."

"It doesn't need to be said." Smiling, I continue. "You're making his decision that much easier. He knows, as do I, that with you operating the mercantile he has the biggest load off his mind. I'll be free to see Paris. My one regret is that it will be without Walter at my side."

Walter isn't my only regret. That I will never give birth to another child torments me. I can't help myself, my heart aches so, I begin to cry. Emily hugs me. She doesn't speak, nor do I.

There's nothing to say.

TWELVE

Alone on the pier, I'm overcome with emotion. Holding back tears, I do what I've done many times in recent months; I have a silent conversation with Walter.

"Darling, you should be here with me. Why did you have to leave?" If people could hear me, they would think me insane.

"Lura, I'll always be with you. I'm in your heart."

"It's so hard, Walter. Please forgive me. I'm so lonely without you and Little George."

The SS *La Touraine* is a beautiful vessel. Always curious, I read all the brochures and newspaper articles I could find. Four years old, she's one of the largest and fastest ocean liners in the world. Black with white trim, her funnels, bright red, are encircled by black bands at the top of the smokestacks.

I'm almost knocked off my feet as a man and woman rush by me. "Hurry, we need to get aboard." It seems an afterthought as the man mumbles, "Pardon, ma'am." Forced from my musing, I hurry to board the ship.

"Welcome to *La Touraine*, Mrs. Myer. We hope you enjoy your time with us. Your suite is ready. Henri, your butler, has arranged your luggage. He will attend to all your needs."

"Thank you, Captain."

Henri escorts me to the first-class section of the ship. In accented English, he shows me the suite that will be my home for the next seven days. It reminds me of my parent's bedroom suite. There are two bedrooms separated by a salon and a study. The salon is equipped with a fully stocked bar. I can smell the residue of cigar smoke.

I ask Henri to tell me about the ship. He recaps what I already know and then adds, "She is the fifth-largest steamship in the world. She is very fast." Struggling for words, he slips into French. He seems surprised when I answer him in French. Smiling, he tells me that the ship can reach speeds of nineteen knots. Conversing in his native tongue, I ask him to tell me about the other accommodations aboard the ship. I'm surprised to learn that *La Touraine* has spaces for almost eleven hundred passengers. Third class is by far the largest with six hundred rooms. Those passengers are forward and aft. They have a small area set for walking with a view of the ocean.

"We have three undred and ninety-two first-class suites. Yours is the largest. In addition to me, you have a personal maid, Monique. If you desire her or my services at any time, you need only ring for us."

"When shall I meet Monique?"

Before Henri can answer, there's a knock at the door. "That should be her, Madame."

Opening the door, Henri ushers in a young Negro woman with skin the color I've heard referred to as high yellow. She doesn't appear to be older than sixteen. "Madame, this is Monique. She will be at your service throughout the voyage to France."

She curtsies. "Madame. I'm pleased to be at your service." She speaks English with an inflection unfamiliar to me. It isn't typical French, and I ask her about the accent. I'm surprised by her answer.

"I'm Algerian. I came to France with the help of my father's cousin, Monsieur Jules-Martin Carbon, the Governor-General."

"Your father's cousin is a famous politician."

"I will leave you two to become acquainted," Henri says as he backs to the cabin door and slips away.

"Madame, it is of no importance. I'm available whenever you wish for my services. If you have nothing for me, I will leave and return later to assist you in preparing for dinner."

The rapid departure of Henri, followed by that of Monique, seems odd. Once they leave, I sit before the vanity. Brushing out my hair, I'm overcome by melancholy—renewed despair at the loss of my loved ones. I fight to reclaim control of my mind and body. I don't appreciate that tears are clouding my vision, my nose is running, and there is a deep ache in my chest. Looking down, I see that I'm rubbing Mother's pendant between my hands.

I feel Walter's presence, his words clear. "You must not allow melancholia to overtake you. Do not allow it to confine you to the prison from which Emily freed you."

Looking in the mirror, I smile as I point at the reflection. "Walter's right. I will not allow you to drag me down. Now, get dressed for dinner."

I'm in a good mood, but not strong enough to eat alone. I decide that I'll eat all dinners with companions for the seven evenings aboard *La Touraine*. Dinners during which I shall ignore my pain and concentrate on my companions.

I summon Monique, who helps me select the proper attire for dinner. Her selection, a floor-length dress of light green velvet, is perfect. When she finishes dressing me and takes her leave, Henri returns.

"Henri, how does one determine when and with whom one shall dine, particularly a widow traveling alone?"

Henri has an easy and comfortable way about him. We converse as if he has been my confidant and servant for many years.

"Does Madame wish friendly and entertaining

conversation? Or is Madame looking for something, ah, shall we say, more involved?"

"Ah, Henri, you are a rascal."

CROSSING THE ATLANTIC FOR THE FIRST TIME IS less exciting than I expected. Once the New York skyline falls below the western horizon, the one change in scenery is watching the sunset. My second full day at sea finds me reading and napping on the crowded promenade. The sea calm, the sun bright, I dozed. I believe I slept for an hour or two before lunch and again afterward. The months of stress and then the rush to get Mr. Bartolini and Mr. Brandeis in my service have taken a toll. I'm exhausted.

Waking the morning of my third day at sea, I notice that my stateroom is still dark. Looking at my clock, I see it's 4:00 a.m., and I'm wide-awake. Whatever shall I do?

It dawns on me that sunrise must be spectacular at sea. Hurrying, I dress and rush to the promenade deck. I'm not alone. The forward deck is crowded with first-class passengers.

"*Madame, voudriez-vous pour une tasse de chocolat chaud?*" a voice asks in French.

"I would prefer coffee if it's available," I answer in English.

"*Mais naturellement, Madame.*" Within minutes, a steward hands me a mug of steaming coffee. The fragrance drifts upward. Gripping the cup with both hands, I bring it close to my face, near my nose, and inhale the aroma. The combination is uplifting and tantalizing, with a hint of cloves, maybe even cinnamon. The sensation is so unique that I fear I'll be disappointed by the taste. I'm not. It's exquisite.

When the server returns, I do something a lady rarely does; I ask for a second cup. "This coffee is wonderful. What is the secret?"

"Merano is our secret, Madame."

"What? You must tell me."

"Merano is a small town in South Tyrol, in Northern Italy. A local businessman, Josef Schreyogg, fetches coffees from all over the world. He has perfected a blend for *La Touraine*. We have exclusive rights to this coffee. Is it not wonderful?"

"Yes, it certainly is."

A page rings his bell and announces that sunrise will be in five minutes. There's a flurry of activity as we all try to move into the best position. I'm blocked in by a large woman and her even more rotund escort. "Excuse me, may I pass?"

The man grunts, the woman sniffs and raises her face, but neither move. I'm trapped behind them by the people to my sides and back. Resigned to missing the event, I start to retreat. Someone takes my right arm. What is this? All I see is the back of a tall man. He's wearing a dark bowler and a black topcoat. With his right arm, he grabs the rotund man by the shoulder and spins him away. In a soft, but firm voice, he says, "Step aside for the lady." Not looking my way, the stranger bulls his way to the railing, where he deposits me and leaves without another word. I have no idea who my benefactor is, not even how he looks.

Experiencing an odd sense of familiarity, I wonder what happened. I don't have time to think about it or look for the stranger. There's a shout, "Look, look at the horizon. The sun is coming up."

"Look, here it comes," someone shouts, and I stare far to the front of the ship.

I see the beginning of sunrise, a yellow glow that changes to orange as the sun breaks free of the darkness and moves above the horizon. As the sun peeks out, brilliant rays of light reach ever farther into the sky. As it rises ever higher, the sea between the ship and the horizon turns from raven black to a dark blue-gray.

With each passing moment, the world becomes lovelier, and even though it's my imagination, I begin to feel warmer—strengthened—as if reborn. As the sun reaches far into the sky, and into my heart, the last remnants of despair fly from my soul. Oh, what a splendid and glorious moment this is. The sun hasn't only announced a new day, it has proclaimed a new life—mine.

Within the hour, the sky turns an intense blue, and the water becomes bright blue-tinged with tiny points of white where the wind blows the peaks of the small waves into a froth.

I watch the sunrise each of the remaining days at

sea. Despite the splendor and brilliance of each occurrence, I don't relive the wonder of that first morning. Nor do I notice the stranger who had appeared when needed.

I can't explain it, but somehow, I feel disappointed.

THIRTEEN

IT'S A BEAUTIFUL MORNING WHEN I FIRST CATCH sight of the outer port of Le Havre. Still somewhat chilly on that June 1894 day. It strikes me that five months have passed since the horrible accident robbed me of Walter and Little George. Forcing the memory from my thoughts, I paint this new scene in my mind. I want to remember this, my first glimpse of Europe, of France. Even before the harbor comes into view, there are changes. As more Seagulls appear, the sea changes from a shade of sapphire to a murky brown. The transformation is abrupt. There's a line visible in the water. The filth is evident for at least a half hour before we gain sight of land.

The opening to the port is narrower than New York. As we approach the entrance, the ship slows to a crawl as dinky boats crisscross her path. Many small sailboats ply the water. Most must be fishing boats as they have nets hanging from racks. With one exception, all but the largest ships appear to be in advanced stages of deterioration. As we ease into our berth, a yacht flying a British ensign heads out of the port. The vessel is immaculate in its white with red trim. Several crewmen are visible hustling about the decks in bright blue uniforms.

Maybe I should have gone to England.

I hope the city isn't as depressing as the port. It proves to be far worse.

Waiting to disembark, I see an oddly familiar figure leaving the end of the gangplank and stepping on the pier. Is it the stranger?

The man turns and appears to be scanning the first-class promenade. I can't be positive, but I'm sure he halts his search and stares at me for a moment. I move closer to the railing to get a better view. He must discern from my movement my intention for he drops his head to his chest, turns, and hurries from sight.

Will I see him again?

The ship has my baggage delivered to the railway station and stowed aboard the train. There's a cab waiting when I leave the ship. The train will not wait, and there's no time to look about the city. Had I taken an extra day and stayed over in Le Havre, my life may not have undergone the upheaval that became my greatest adventure.

The first and last hours of the otherwise

uneventful eight-hour train ride from Le Havre to Paris are dreary and disturbing. The filth, both human and the land, were beyond anything I've ever experienced. By the time I leave the train, I am dirty and on the verge of being ill.

The farmland between the cities is much the same as the country between Connecticut and New York. The differences are the farms themselves. Ancient rock fences, many falling, abound in the French countryside. The fields, and I assume the farms, are much smaller than in America. I soon learn that everything in France, except the recently completed Eiffel Tower, is smaller.

For my lodgings in Paris, I chose one of the smaller and less public hotels. As I explained to Emily before departure, "I want my privacy to come and go as an ordinary tourist." Mr. Bartolini wanted me to hire a traveling companion and a bodyguard. I rejected his advice. Staying as inconspicuous as possible in a small hotel is my one concession to their worries.

My suite at the hotel is smaller than the one I enjoyed aboard *La Touraine*.

FOURTEEN

After two days rest, I contact Cook Travel
Agency and arrange for a driver. Among the several
places I plan to visit, the Louvre is at the top of the
list, followed closely by the Eiffel Tower. The travel
agency has an excellent reputation for providing
foreign tourists with quality service.

My driver, Claude Lafournais, a gruff Parisian,
isn't what I expected from Cook. Much taller than the
average Frenchman, he's at least four inches more
than six feet, his face concealed behind a dark beard.
He knows the city well and is an excellent driver. I'm
glad for that. Before we reach the Arc de Triomphe,
I see at least three out-of-control carriages and cabs.
On the Avenue du Bois de Boulogne, a cab collides
with an electric bus right before my eyes. The driver
is thrown clear; the couple sitting behind him is

hurled under the bus. The bus rear wheels run over the woman's legs. One is severed, and blood spews on the tracks. The carnage ignites memories of New York. I cry and shake. Claude pulls off the avenue and stops.

"*Madame, ce qui est la question?*"

"The accident has upset me," I answer in English. "I'm sorry.

Claude asks if I need to rest.

"Please, yes. If we could sit for a few minutes." He stops at a small sidewalk café, leads the way to a sheltered table, and orders Chartreuse for me.

"Madame, I shall return in half-hour's time."

On returning, he gives me a questioning look to which I reply, "I'm fine. Please continue our tour."

The afternoon is fast approaching. Once we circle and pass beneath the Arc de Triomphe, we hurry on to the Louvre. "You have only enough time to visit the *Mona Lisa*. I will bring you back tomorrow so that you can see the *Venus de Milo* and other masterpieces."

I follow his suggestion and hurry to the *Mona Lisa*. It's all I had hoped—beyond my ability to describe. I stand transfixed before the beauty. I'm not alone. Leaning against the barrier are two young girls, both dressed in identical pastel green dresses. Each has long dark hair worn down in the way of young American and Irish girls with a ribbon of matching green tied in a bow. I would think them twins except one is two or three inches shorter than the other.

They remain in the same position with their backs to me for the entire time I view the *Mona Lisa*. They talk in subdued tones. They are speaking English, but I'm not so interested that I bother listening.

My driver approaches. "Madame, the museum will close in a few minutes. You should come now."

Glancing once more at the painting and the two girls, I say, "*Oui, Monsieur.*"

Returning to my hotel, I'm exhausted. "I wish to start later in the day tomorrow. Would you be so kind as to pick me up in the afternoon?"

"If it pleases Madame, I will call for you at two."

"That will be fine."

The hotel has a small dining room, but I'm not up to dining in public. The concierge honors my request and has a fine meal and an excellent wine delivered to my suite. After a leisurely meal, I read. Before the tour, I had wandered the neighborhood and found a small bookshop. Floor to ceiling shelves, filled with leather-bound volumes, cover the walls. I'm in France, so I shall work on my French, including my ability to read. I purchased a copy of Victor Hugo's *Les Misérables*. What better story to read while in Paris? I fall asleep, struggling with my unpolished translation.

At two, the driver calls for me. After a casual ride through the avenues, we pass the *Colonne Vendôme* where several Cook Travel Agency carriages sit while their passengers wander about admiring the column and the many fine hotels surrounding the *Place*

Vendôme. After a ride past other tourist attractions, Claude deposits me at the entrance to the Louvre. "Madame, I shall return in two hours if it pleases you."

"That will be fine. I shall return to this spot in two hours."

If I'm to see the *Venus de Milo*, the works of Raphael, and enjoy some further time with the *Mona Lisa*, I must hurry. As I turn to the entrance, two very brutish and filthy men block my path. Both smell of fish, stale wine, and urine. They remind me of bullies; there's an air of anger about them. Almost overcome by fright, I resolve not to show it.

"*Avez-vous besoin d'un guide?*" The shorter of the two asks in French if I need a guide.

I endeavor to ignore him by saying, "I don't speak French," as I step around the pair.

The man persists. "It is my pleasure to speak the Eng-gah-leash and to assist you as a guide." He sneers and says to his companion in vulgar French, "This cow will be easy. We shall have her jewels and money within the hour."

"I must insist that you leave me alone. Go away." They pay no attention as they continue blocking my path. Suddenly they turn away and hurry out of sight. Turning around, I expect to see a Gendarme. There's none in sight. Moving away and disappearing into the crowd, I see the back of a man. He's wearing a bowler and a dark topcoat. Could it be the stranger?

I make my way into the museum. The crowds

are lighter than yesterday. Entering the chamber containing the *Mona Lisa*, I'm shocked to see the same two young girls sitting on a bench across the gallery from the painting. The taller girl, whom I assume to be older, is sitting to the left, her hands clasped in front. The shorter one is leaning against her. She appears to be asleep.

Why, they are wearing the same dresses as yesterday. They are soiled and rumpled as if they have slept in their clothing. Their hair is unwashed and in need of brushing. Should I approach them?

My dilemma is answered when the shorter of the two sits up, turns, and stares at me. My Lord, the poor child is frightened. Her lips are trembling so. If it were not warm in here, I would suspect that she was cold. Her voice quivers as she whispers, "Katie."

The taller girl turns and stands up next to the other. She seems frightened as she takes the other girl's hand into hers. The shorter one, eyes wet and watery, is whimpering. She isn't what I expected. She must be older than her taller companion. There is no question in my mind; the girls are sisters.

"My name is Lura." I kneel before them. "Please don't be frightened. Are you alone? Where are your parents?"

The shorter one cries uncontrollably. I reach out to her.

"Leave my sister alone," the taller one says in a shrill voice as she steps between us. She takes a deep breath, crosses her arms, and adds, "We're fine."

Thank goodness, they speak English.

The shorter one speaks. "No, we're not Katie. Father isn't coming back."

Katie's bravado seems to abandon her. By getting down to their level, eye to eye, I seem to have reduced their fear. "Girls, maybe I can help. There's a bench against the back wall. Why don't we sit there and talk?"

The girls exchange looks. Katie maintains a semblance of defiance. The other girl nods as I speak. Turning to her sister, I can barely hear, "Please, Katie, oh, please. I'm so scared. Please let the lady help us." Reluctantly, Katie moves to the bench. She doesn't relinquish her sister's hand, even as they sit. I don't want to frighten them. Rising, I sit a foot away from the older girl.

"Didn't I see you girls here yesterday?"

The girls look exhausted. "Yes. Our papa brought us here to see her."

"Her?"

The shorter girl points at the *Mona Lisa*. "Father wanted us to see her. He says she's the most beautiful woman in the world."

"Father sat here on this bench with us for a long time. Then he took us to the rail so that we could see her up close," Katie adds.

Katie's sister is coming to life; her fear seems to dissipate as she talks. "After we looked at her for a long time, two men came and talked to Papa. After they left, he said he had to talk to someone. He told us to wait here for him, but he didn't come back."

"Have you been here in the museum since yesterday?"

"No," the girls answer in chorus.

"Where'd you go? Where'd you spend the night?"

Katie takes a deep breath and lets out an audible sigh before answering. "We saw you yesterday. After you left, the guide told us the museum was closing, and we had to leave."

"Have you seen your father since he left you here yesterday?"

"No, we don't know where he is." Ada Mae is again crying.

"What did you do when you left here?"

Katie takes the lead. "We tried to find our hotel, but we don't remember the name. So, we walked and walked. When it was dark, we were hungry. We saw a lady pushing a baby carriage. She didn't speak English. Father gave us each one-hundred franc, and I showed her our money. She smiled and motioned for us to follow her."

"Where did she take you?"

"To her home, a tiny apartment. She gave us a bowl of soup and a piece of bread. Then she took our money and made us leave."

"Oh, my Lord. What a terrible woman."

"We didn't leave. I pounded on her door until she opened it. She shook her fist at us and talked loudly. I shook my head no, put my hands together, and showed her we wanted to sleep. She yelled, but then she took us into the kitchen. We slept on the floor," Katie says.

"Were you there all night?"

"Yes, but she made us leave in the morning."

The girls explain that the woman took all their money but didn't give them breakfast, not even a slice of bread.

"If you have no money, how did you get back in here?"

Katie smiles. "We saw a group of children being brought inside by some grownups, so we followed them in. No one asked us for a ticket."

Although the girls remain frightened, I convince them to come with me. "My driver will be out front. Please come with me, and we shall eat. You can't stay here, the museum is closing." Hunger overcomes fear.

As we enter the carriage, I notice the same two scoundrels who had accosted me earlier. They glare in my direction from the corner of a kiosk. The older one shakes a fist at me before hammering it against the wall where he stands.

My heart racing, I take a deep breath and force myself to be calm. I can't telegraph my fear to the girls. They're frightened enough already without adding my dread to theirs.

CLAUDE DOESN'T SEEM SURPRISED OR CONCERNED when I bring the two girls to the carriage. He doesn't ask any questions when I say, "Please return to the hotel."

After depositing us at the hotel, he asks, "Will Madame have further need for my services?"

"Don't you have other duties to attend to at Cook Travel?"

"Work is slow, and I have nothing on my schedule for the next few days."

I think about the girls. I can provide for them tonight, but I must locate their father in the morning. "I would like you to return at ten tomorrow morning. Please adjust your schedule and plan on being at my service for the next two or three days. Is that acceptable?"

"I will be here at ten."

"Please notify the concierge when you arrive. I will call him when ready."

"Would you girls like to eat in my rooms? We can talk about your father and what we must do to locate him."

Both girls agree. I order an American style meal for three. Knowing how hungry they must be, I don't order the child's portion. It's the right decision as the girls clean their plates while I leave half my meal. Dessert disappears in the blink of an eye.

Dinner ended, I want to talk about their father and how we might find him. It isn't to be. Finished with dessert, the girls exhibit signs of exhaustion. I put them in the second bedroom. Removing their dresses, I realize they have no nightclothes.

"We'll be alright, Miss Lura." As soon as their heads collapse on the pillow, they are asleep.

Alone in the sitting room, worry overtakes me. "Whatever shall I do with these children? How can we find their father?" I fret into the wee hours and fall asleep in the chair.

The summer sun shining through the window wakes me. I have time to dress before the girls arise. They come into the drawing room in the dresses that show the wear of three days.

"Girls, we must do something about your clothes. You can't run around dressed like wild animals."

I ring for the concierge. "Please send me a maid, preferably one with children. I will require her services for a few hours."

The maid is a mother with several children. I explain that we need undergarments, nightclothes, and dresses for the girls. "Can you find a store and purchase these items?"

"But of course, Madame. *La Grands Magasins Dufayel* is a huge department store with what you need for the children. If I can get transportation, I can travel there and buy what you desire, and at a reasonable cost."

"My driver will be here at ten, and he shall take you. Here are enough francs for what we wish. Please also get a valise for each of the girls."

The girls and I enjoy breakfast while the maid makes arrangements to be away. Finished eating, I ask the girls to tell me about their hotel and their father. I also ask, "Where is your mother?"

My question visibly shakes Katie. Her eyes redden, she stares down at her hands as tears appear at the edge of her eyes. Ada Mae gets up and goes to her sister. She puts her arms around her as she says, "Don't cry." Turning to me, she says, "Our mother died when Katie was two."

I'm unable to control my emotions as the thought of Little George fills my heart. I'm crying and rubbing Mother's pendant. Bending over, the all too familiar ache returns to my chest. I feel myself falling back into the cage of depression I thought I had left behind in America. Arms wrap around me.

"It's alright, Miss Lura. Mama's in heaven. Please don't cry. We'll help you." Two small voices comfort me.

These poor darlings have no mother, their father has disappeared, and they are comforting me. The affection they show me brings me back from the abyss of despair. I must be strong for them.

My heart is still acting oddly. The ache is gone replaced by a beating that reminds me of the joy I felt when Walter asked for my hand in marriage. For some unknown reason, I feel responsible for the girls and want to keep them safe. Pulling myself together, I hug the two and thank them. "Girls, we have to make plans."

They seem perplexed, as one, they ask, "What plans?" I come to accept and expect their simultaneous speech. At first, it seems wondrous, but as we grow together, I understand it is another revelation of the close bond they share.

"Before we begin our search for your father, there are a few things I need to know. First, what's your last name?"

"I'm Ada Mae Dean. I'm twelve years old."

"I'm Catherine Margaret Dean. I'm ten, and I'm bigger than my big sister."

"What's your father's name, and where do you live?"

"Francis Patrick Dean. We lived in Boston before we came to Paris."

Over the next few hours, the girls tell me about their father and their life in Boston. They know little of his life outside their home. I decide to send Mr. Brandeis a telegraph requesting an inquiry into the business of Mr. Dean. Katie's too young to remember her mother. The death of their mother brought a series of nannies. All with children of their own, none of whom stayed with the girls for more than a year.

Before we can talk further, the maid returns with new clothes. The girls are excited and want to change. "No. Young ladies must be clean, and without the odors you carry on your body, especially in new outfits."

"Madame is correct. I will prepare baths for the

young ladies and then help them dress," the maid volunteers.

Ada Mae is indignant. "I can bathe and dress. I don't need your help."

"Oh, don't be such a prude, Ada Mae." Before she can answer, Katie throws off her dirty clothes and runs to the bedroom.

WHEN THE GIRLS ARE BATHED AND DRESSED, I have them tell me everything they can about their hotel. Armed with my notes, we call for the carriage. I tell Claude that we are looking for a certain hotel and give him a description based upon what the girls have told me. Before going down to the carriage, we agreed that Claude didn't need to know the reason for our search.

"Does Madame wish to tell me why we're looking for this particular hotel?"

As politely as I can, I tell Claude it isn't his business. He's always gruff, so I can't tell if he takes offense.

"There are several hotels that match your description. If Madame approves, I will go to the one closest to the Louvre first."

"Why there?"

"Madame and the young ladies met at the Louvre."

"Very well, that's an excellent idea."

"May I make another suggestion that might please the young ladies?"

"And what might that be?"

"Our route will take us near the *Boulevard de la Madeleine*. A short detour will take us to the finest candy store in Paris."

The girls assure me that such a brief detour will in no way interfere with the search for their father. A short while later, the girls, Claude, and I are pulling on French Chew, a new type of candy.

"Chew is a good name for this sweet chewy candy," I tell the girls.

After viewing four hotels, the girls are feeling the loneliness brought on by their father's absence. Ada Mae's on the verge of tears. Her eyes redden as she becomes sullen. Katie holds Ada Mae, looks furtively at passersby, and slumps down in the carriage seat, all belying the bravado that she tries miserably to portray.

"Madame, if I may, perhaps you should take the children to La Sûreté. They have detectives experienced in such matters."

"I'm not surprised that Claude has concluded that the girl's father is missing. He may be right. I am, after all, a woman alone in a foreign country. How can I best help these children?

"What's La Sûreté?" Katie sits up, alert.

"La Sûreté is the national police. They have many detectives who can help you young ladies find your papa."

Ada Mae will have nothing to do with the police.

"Papa doesn't like the police. He always tells us

to stay away from them. He says they are worse than the hooligans."

"Your father may be right. But if the ladies can forgive me, you need help."

I make a decision. "We can worry about the police later. For now, please return us to the hotel."

"As you wish, Madame."

FIFTEEN

BEFORE WE BEGAN OUR SEARCH THAT AFTERNOON, I sent a telegraph to Mr. Brandeis. I didn't expect an answer for a day or two. I'm surprised when the concierge hands me an envelope.

As much as I want to tear it open and read the response, I remind myself that the girls are having a very difficult time. They miss their father terribly. I know all too well how that feels and how it can drive one to despair.

"Girls, let's retire to our rooms and refresh ourselves."

I ask the concierge, "Is the maid who helped us this morning on the premises?"

"Yes, Madame. Would you like me to send her to you?"

The maid comes to the suite and prepares the bed for the girls and brushes out their hair while I read Mr. Brandeis's telegram. The response surprises me, both for the speed in which he answers and in the information it contains.

June 5, 1894
Mrs. Lura Myer

Francis Patrick Dean is a known Boston criminal, a member of the Irish Mob. Has been suspected in several mob killings of Italian Mafia. Attempting to seize power in the Boston underworld. A new Irish gang, the Winter Hill Irish Mob, is growing in power in Boston. Sources reveal that Francis Dean has been trying to distance himself from the gangs. Police surmise that he has fled the country as the result of two contracts on his life, one by his old gang, and the other by the Winter Hill Irish Mob. Might I ask as to the nature of your inquiry?

Louis Brandeis

I respond to Mr. Brandeis with a plea that he arrange for a detective in Paris to assist me in a confidential matter of the greatest importance. I make no mention of the girls.

I end the telegram with, "Mr. Brandeis, this is a matter requiring the greatest discretion. Please forgive my reticence in providing any further details."

Once I complete the draft of my plea, I place it away, out of sight, in the writing desk. I believe the girls to be asleep but decide to check on them before

I retire. Opening the door to their bedchamber, I hear muffled sounds. One of the girls is weeping, and the other comforts her. Both have pulled the bedcovers over them. I'm surprised to recognize the two voices well enough to know that Ada Mae's crying, as Katie tries to soothe her.

Not wanting to surprise or startle them, I knock on the doorframe and speak, "Girls, it's me, Lura. May I come in?"

After a moment, I repeat my entreaty somewhat louder. This time there's a response from Katie. "Oh, please do, Miss Lura." Away go the covers as the two sit up. Ada Mae's trying desperately to cover the fact that she has been crying.

I give her a moment to compose herself before sitting at her side on the bed.

"How are you girls doing?"

"We're worried about Papa. We haven't seen him for days. He never left us alone before. Do you think something happened to him?" Katie says.

Showing more conviction than I feel, I say, "I'm sure that your father is alright and will be back tomorrow. We should go to the Louvre and wait near the *Mona Lisa* for him in the morning." Both girls seemed relieved when I suggest this. They and I so much want to believe it to be true. I know their father is an evil man; I fear that something terrible has happened to him. He may be evil, but I believe he loves these girls.

"Then it's settled. Once we have breakfast,

Claude shall take us to find your father."

Both girls speak at once. "Thank you, Miss Lura."

"Now, I shall read you a story if you promise to go right to sleep."

"Father used to read to us," says Katie. "What will you read?"

One of the books I bought to help brush up on my French is a translation of *Little Women* by one of my favorite authors, Louisa May Alcott.

"I will begin reading you the story of four sisters growing up in America."

FOR REASONS I CAN'T EXPLAIN, NOR UNDERSTAND, I'm reluctant to notify the authorities either here in France or Boston. My decision proves to be providential.

The next day I fear using the hotel staff to post the message risks notification of La Sûreté. I'll wait and have Claude take me to the telegraph office.

When Claude arrives to take us to the Louvre, I order him to detour to the telegraph office. While he waits with the carriage, I take the girls with me into the office. This proves to be more difficult than I imagined.

"Madame, for me to accept your telegraph, you must, in addition to the fee, provide us with your name and the name of the hotel at which you are staying. Otherwise, we cannot accept your message."

After several minutes, a hand touches my shoulder, turning, Claude signals me to follow him.

"Madame, if you wish to bypass the customary regulations, you must provide the woman with additional motivation."

"What motivation?"

"Does Madame have a twenty-franc note?"

"I do. Why do you ask?" Even as I say the words, I know what Claude is telling me. "Thank you, Claude."

Returning to the window, the same woman says, "How may I help Madame?"

Placing a twenty-franc note below the written message, I hand both to her.

"Yes, Madame, I believe we have all we need to send your telegraph. I hope Madame has a pleasant morning."

Returning with the girls to the carriage, I whisper, "Thank You." Claude smiles as he helps us into the carriage.

WE SPEND SEVERAL HOURS ON THE BENCH NEAR the *Mona Lisa*. Mr. Dean has been missing for three days. After a dreadful lunch, we return and remain until the museum closes. The girls are disheartened. I try to cheer them up.

"May I suggest that we again detour to the *Boulevard de la Madeleine*? We could stop at the candy store and get more of that wonderful French Chew."

Even the promise of candy does nothing to bring the girls out of their sad malaise.

Entering our hotel, the concierge comes to me. "Madame, a gentleman is waiting in the lobby for you. He has been here for several hours."

"Do you know who he is or what he wants?"

"No, Madame. I asked him the same questions. He refused to tell me anything other than he will wait for your arrival."

"Thank you. Will you give him a message for me?"

"But of course."

"Please tell him I will join him in the lobby in thirty minutes."

Thirty minutes later, the girls are ensconced in our room with the maid. She's telling them stories of life in Paris.

As I enter the lobby, a short dark man rises from one of the couches. Clean-shaven, he's shorter than me but with a look of strength. His clothes are fashionable but threadbare. He looks worn.

"Madame Myer?"

"Yes. What can I do for you?"

He looks around the room before speaking. There are no others in the lobby. "Monsieur Brandeis sent me. My name is Emil Benoit."

"What are your instructions?"

"I'm to help you locate a gentleman and provide any further assistance you wish."

"How are you to be paid?"

"Monsieur Brandeis made arrangements. I'm well paid for my services."

Mr. Benoit is one of those men that would go unnoticed in almost any situation. This works well for him and for my needs.

"What do you know of the man that you are to find."

"Nothing."

I spend the next ten minutes telling Mr. Benoit everything I've learned about Francis Dean, with one exception; I don't tell him I have the girls. I do mention that Mr. Dean was traveling with two young girls, his daughters.

"This is a great deal of information. It would be much more useful if we knew how and when he arrived and which hotel he used."

I hadn't thought to ask the girls about their travel arrangements. I was not about to risk their safety by telling Mr. Benoit to wait while I went to the rooms and asked. "I may be able to obtain some information regarding Mr. Dean's method of transportation tomorrow. How can I contact you?"

Handing me a card, he says, "You may leave a message for me at this location." The card has an address listed with no name. Because Mr. Brandeis sent the man, I don't question his abilities.

"When shall I hear from you, Mr. Benoit?"

"Unless an emergency arises, I will present myself to you here tomorrow at two in the afternoon. Does that meet with Madame's satisfaction?"

"It does. I shall see you then."

Returning to my suite, I find that the maid has ordered dinner for the girls and me. There is more than we can eat. I ask her to join us. She's embarrassed, "But no, Madame. It isn't allowed, nor is it proper." The girls will have none of her excuses and drag her to the table. She is pleasant company and regales us with tales of life in Paris.

THE COLD AND DREARY MORNING DOESN'T BEGIN well. Before the first hint of dawn, I wake to the sound of muffled sobs. Beneath their covers, I find Ada Mae comforting Katie. Both have tears in their eyes.

"Katie, what's wrong? Why are you crying?"

"She's scared. So am I. Has something terrible happened to Papa?" Ada Mae's the one who answers.

I can't answer, for I don't know. Although I fear the girls' father murdered, I must not show my concern lest they become even more frightened. I bring them into my bed and nestle them in my arms. Smelling of lavender and spice from their evening bath and exhausted, within minutes they have cried themselves to sleep. Sharing their fears, I silently cry myself to sleep. Waking hours later, the girls seem to be in better spirits. We remain in bed for most of the morning.

After a late breakfast of fruit, croissants, chocolate for the girls, and coffee for me, we are tired of being confined to the room. Even though they are still worried about their father, the girls are full of energy.

"Miss Lura, we must go outside, or surely we'll explode."

"I don't believe I've ever seen a young lady explode. Maybe I should keep you two inside, so I can witness this most wondrous event." The girls fill the room with gales of laughter.

I'm loath to walk about the streets of Paris unaccompanied. I can't get the memory of the two men who accosted me at the Louvre out of my mind. Clasping Mother's pendant, I agree to a walk with one requirement. "I will send for Claude. If he can accompany us, then we shall walk."

I ring for the concierge who sends a messenger to Cook Travel Agency. They are more than happy to send an otherwise unoccupied driver to escort us.

"I'm a carriage driver, not a walker of ladies, and most assuredly not a bodyguard," Claude protests in his usual gruff persona. By now, both the girls and I know he's a gentle bear with a loud growl, but no bite. Bowing so that his head almost touches the floor, he asks the girls, "And where would the *juenes dames* care to walk on this lovely day?"

Laughing, both hug him and say, "The candy store." Shaking the girls playfully, he reminds them that it is much too far for walking. "I will find you another candy store where Madame Myer shall purchase enough French Chew for all of us."

"Miss Lura, do you think we will find our papa today?" Ada Mae asks before I can ponder what news the day will bring.

I look at her with wonder in my heart. How these two children can endure this pain is beyond me. I squeeze my eyes and take a deep breath before my fear of crying is stifled. "I hope so child. When we return this afternoon, let's pray for good news about your father. But now, let's enjoy this beautiful day."

The day is clear and warm. Even as we walk along the Seine, we're comfortable. Claude takes us to where we can view the *Arc de Triomphe de l'Étoile* while sitting at an outside table of a small café. Still satisfied from breakfast, I have a coffee. The girls, already hungry, share a sweet pastry.

"Will you have room for French Chew?"

"*Mais bien sûr, Madame,*" Claude answers for them. He spreads his arms and gives me a look of amazement. "Doesn't one always have room for a delicacy such as French Chew?"

As we resume our stroll, I ask Claude about the smaller monument I saw near the Louvre.

"Ah, Madame. You speak of the *Arc de Triomphe du Carrousel.* It is but half the size of this magnificent shrine." He points to the one we are leaving, and says, "It was built to honor the brave men who fought and died for France in *la Révolution* and the wars of Napoléon."

The day is alive with sounds, carriages passing over cobblestoned avenues, couples talking in whispers, and birds in song. The trees in blossom add a sweet perfume that almost, but not quite, covers the smell of sewage flowing down the gutters.

We walk for about an hour before we find a candy store that meets Claude's stringent requirements. Had the girls been in charge, we would have stopped at one of four or five we passed along the way. At each of those, Claude refused the girls admittance, saying, "This imposter of a candy store is no place for ladies such as you."

At each, one or both girls ask, "What's wrong?"

"This is but an imitation of a true maker of French Chew." Shaking his head in disbelief, he continues, "This is not a maker of the wonderful candy. These sheep buy it from the makers and sell it. We will not stop until we come to a shop that not only sells the chew but one that makes it fresh. There is none better."

They could not convince him otherwise.

When we approach an unpretentious candy store, the girls look at him with the question in their eyes, "Well, Monsieur Claude, is this store good enough for you?"

"Follow me, juenes dames. We have finally found a store worthy of your attention."

The girls insist on eating some of the French Chew as we walk back to the hotel. I find their behavior beyond disreputable. They and Claude enjoy my discomfort. I can't stand it any longer. Turning to the girls, I say, "Oh, alright. We are in

Paris, and no one here knows me. Ada Mae, give me a small, very small, piece of that wonderful candy."

I sense—know—we are being followed. I look at Claude. He knows what I fear. Simultaneously, my pace quickens. If I allow my fear to take control—to show—the girls will sense my apprehension and will be frightened.

I must not allow that to happen. Slowing, almost stopping, I bend over and take a large piece of the French Chew from Ada Mae. As I stand, I look back down the walk. I gasp as I see the two men from the Louvre. They're not more than a hundred feet behind us. When I look up, they turn and walk into a shop.

"Claude."

"I know, Madame. You and the girls walk in front of me. We shall go directly to the hotel."

"What is it, Miss Lura?" Katie asks, "Is something wrong?"

"No, darling. We need to return to the hotel so that I can meet with a gentleman."

"Do you mean the detective?"

I've forgotten how bright these girls are. "Yes. Now let's get on about our business. We have no time to dillydally."

Nearing the hotel, Claude motions for me to go ahead with the girls. "I will have a word with the gentlemen."

Inside, I hurry the girls to our suite. I no longer refer to it as my suite, but ours. The girls have become part of my life. How big a part will be a surprise.

Minutes after I close and lock the door, there's a knock.

"Who is it?"

"Claude, Madame."

I hurry to the door and admit him. "What happened? What did you say to those men?"

"It is strange, Madame. I leaned against a wall to wait until the men approached and then confront them. I meant to dissuade them from following you again."

"What was strange?"

"After I waited what I believed to be ample time for them to approach, I looked for them. A man, a stranger, was pushing them back the way they came. He may have struck them."

"Why do you say that?"

"The two were bent over with their arms raised to cover, possibly protect, their heads. I thought to follow, but then they turned a corner. When I got to the corner, they were no longer in sight. *Très étrange.*"

"What did the man look like?"

"He was wearing one of the popular hats. I believe you call it a bowler."

"Was he wearing a dark topcoat?"

"Yes, he was. That struck me as odd. It is very warm today. Why would he have on such a coat?"

I don't tell Claude, but I know who the man is. He's the stranger from the ship and the Louvre. Whatever does this man want? And why does he keep coming to my rescue?

SIXTEEN

THE FOLLOWING AFTERNOON, MY SISTER-IN-LAW IS
out touring the city. Lura, the two girls, and the
carriage driver are walking. I struggle with the
cowardly way I've followed her. I should have come
to her at the time of my brother's death. Now, I can't.
It would paint me as a degenerate intruder, a
perversion. Once she returns to her home, I will
politely introduce myself.

They are eating candy when the two men from
the Louvre appear between them and me. What do
these ne'er-do-wells want?

As we near the hotel, the two men increase their
pace as though they intend to accost the group.
Closing the distance, I grab the two and pull them
into an alley. They shout at me in French. I
understand nothing they say.

"Shut up. Do you speak English?"

"Oui, Monsieur. I speak Eng-gah-leash," the taller one says.

"Why are you following that woman?"

"No, Monsieur. We . . . we follow no one."

"Don't lie. You're the same two who accosted her at the Louvre. Why are you following her?"

"Monsieur is mistaken. We have not seen the Madame before."

I let go of their collars and strike the man. The other cowers as the first tries to strike back at me. I knock him to the ground where he remains. As I turn to the other man, he cringes and drops to the ground next to the first.

"Let this be a warning. If I find you near the woman again, I'll break your bones." Lura's carriage driver is returning, so pushing them ahead, I leave quietly, but rapidly.

SEVENTEEN

"MADAME, MONSIEUR BENOIT IS WAITING IN THE salon," the concierge announces.

"Claude, would you mind waiting with the girls for a few minutes? I have something which I must attend to."

"*Mais naturellement, Madame.* We shall enjoy a bit of delicious French Chew."

"*BONJOUR. MONSIEUR BENOIT.*"

"Madame."

"I have the information you requested about Mr. Dean's mode of travel and when he arrived here."

"It is no longer necessary, Madame, I have located Mr. Dean's hotel. The news I bring is disturbing." He pauses as if to gather his thoughts. "Mr. Dean and two young ladies, much like the two in your company, took a small suite of rooms not far from the railroad station. I have examined the rooms. As I said, the news is disturbing."

"Go on."

"For a small gift, I was able to inspect the rooms. There had been a struggle. I fear it didn't end well. There is a great deal of blood and marks that . . . ah . . . I believe the word is . . . ah . . . indicate a body was wrapped in a rug and taken from the room."

"Oh, my Lord." I fear the worst.

"Yes. For another small gift, the landlord gave me the man's passport." Benoit hands me an American Passport. The picture is of a man who appears to be much like the one described by Katie and Ada Mae. The name on the document is Francis Patrick Dean.

I don't have a passport; they are not required for Americans traveling to European countries although some carry passports for ease of re-entry. Mr. Dean's Irish heritage must have something to do with his having one.

"Madame, there's more troubling news. The police pulled the body of a man from the Seine last night. There was no identification on the body. It was wrapped in a rug."

"Have you seen the body?"

"I thought to report to Madame first. Do you want my inquiry to be public? If so, that will lead La Sûreté to you and the children."

"If Mr. Dean is dead and La Sûreté learns of the

girls, what will become of them?"

"Madame, the officials will take the girls into custody, and either place them in an orphanage or deliver them to the American Embassy. They will investigate to identify relatives to whom the children may be sent."

"And if they have no living relatives?"

"They will be placed for adoption here or in America. It is the law."

"They have no living relatives. I will not allow them to be confined in an orphanage. What can I do that doesn't involve an official inquiry?"

"With Madame's permission, I will call upon a friend at the morgue tonight. For a small gift, *Mon Ami* will allow a short visit with the body of the man pulled from the Seine. I will take the passport with me to help with the identification. There will be no record of my visit."

"Would you be able to obtain a photograph of the body?"

"It will necessitate another small gift."

"Do you need money from me?"

"No, that is unnecessary. Monsieur Brandeis provided me a generous retainer that more than covers all the . . . ah . . . shall we say gifts? I have provided Monsieur Brandeis with my services in the past. I have no concerns about money."

Mr. Brandeis continues to amaze me.

"When will you report to me concerning this body?"

"Would ten tomorrow morning be too early for Madame?"

"Can you meet me here at eight? I would like to hear your report before the girls awake."

"Eight is excellent, Madame."

"Good. I will see you then." Mr. Benoit rises and directs a small bow in my direction. As he turns, I stop him, "Mr. Benoit."

"Yes, Madame."

"Thank you. You don't know how much I appreciate what you're doing. It is no small matter for me."

"Do not concern yourself, Madame. It is my pleasure. *Bonne journée.*"

ONCE CLAUDE LEAVES, THE GIRLS POUNCE UPON me. They demand to know, "Who is that man Miss Lura? What did he want?"

"Girls, girls, please, it doesn't concern you." I hate lying to them, but until Mr. Benoit reports, I don't want to break their hearts or give them false hope. "Now, what shall we do for dinner?"

Although exhausted, we elect to eat in our hotel's small dining room. Sitting at the smallest of the four tables, we order lamb stew with warm croissants.

Katie again asks me about their father. "Did that man know anything about our papa, Miss Lura?"

"No, he didn't. Now, we must eat while our dinner's warm." I'm overcome with despair but manage to appear calm. My heart aches.

Ada Mae is beyond exhausted as she falls asleep over dessert. Katie pokes her. "Ada Mae, wake up. You're embarrassing Miss Lura."

Rubbing her eyes, Ada Mae raises her head and says, "I'm sorry. I can't help it. I'm tired."

"Come, girls, let's return to our suite. It's time for bed."

The girls are so tired, they ask to go to bed without bathing. Once they're in their nightgowns, Katie calls me in to say good night.

"Ada Mae's almost asleep. Please make her stay up long enough to say our prayers and ask God to bring Father back to us."

My heart is breaking with sorrow for what will surely be the last day that the girls can hold onto the hope that their father's alive. "Yes, let us pray." Both join me at the side of the bed. With one on each side, I say, "Who shall lead us in prayer tonight?"

"I'm too tired," Ada Mae says.

Katie says, "Please, Miss Lura. God might listen to you and help us find our papa."

I've grown to adore the girls in these few days. Releasing a sigh, I put my arms around their shoulders and pull them close. How can I lie to them? And praying for the safe return of their father when I'm sure he's dead is a lie—the worst kind of falsehood.

"Maybe we can all say a silent prayer together." The girls each put an arm around me and squeeze. I know at that instant. It's more than adoration; I love them.

I will do whatever I must to protect them.

"MADAME MYER, THE BODY IN THE MORGUE, IS that of Mr. Dean. *Je suis désolé.*"

"Are you positive?"

"Although the man had been beaten and in the water for many hours, I'm positive it is Monsieur Dean. It is the same man pictured in the passport photograph." He hesitates, "There is more."

"What do you mean, there's more?"

"Might I ask, are the *deux jeunes dames* named Katie and Ada Mae?"

"Yes, they are. Why?"

"There were many tattoos on the body. Two suggest he is the father of the jeunes dames. Over his heart was the word "Ada Mae" and above his right breast, "Katie.""

I'm squeezing Mother's pendant so hard, it's a wonder it doesn't break apart. Tears struggle to erupt from my eyes. I turn away from Mr. Benoit as the tears break free, and a moan escapes from within.

"Madame, may I be of assistance?"

"I'm sorry. Please forgive my bad manners. Give me a moment."

Mr. Benoit produces a handkerchief and hands it to me before getting a glass of water. Sufficiently settled to talk, I ask, "Can the children see him?"

"That would not be wise, Madame. His face was beaten quite severely."

"What will become of the body?"

"If no one claims it, it will be buried in a pauper's grave."

Leaving their father's remains in France would be one more indignity that should be avoided if possible. I resolve to prevent that.

"Can you arrange to have the body claimed and shipped to America?"

"Yes, but many questions will be asked, and the officials may learn of the existence of the jeunes dames." Before I can ask what type of questions, Benoit adds, "There is also the matter of the murderers."

"What about the murderers?"

"They might have an interest in eliminating jeunes dames as possible witnesses to the killing of Monsieur Dean."

"We must keep the girls well hidden."

"La Sûreté will want to know why his daughters have not been located. They will attempt to question the person—you, Madame—who wishes to make the arrangements to remove his body. La Sûreté will have many questions as to what you have done with the girls. Regardless of your intentions, the authorities would be . . . ah, how you say, *obligatoire?*"

"Required is the English word, but I understand. Go on."

"Required to notify the American Embassy. I'm

sure the Americans would take custody of the body and the girls." After a pause, he adds, "Madame would be in danger of being arrested for taking—kidnapping—the children."

"Is there another—more discreet—possibility?"

"Except for La Sûreté, with the presentation of a few small gifts, arrangements can be made."

"Please make the arrangements. Return this afternoon. Come at three. I'll have a bank draft for you. Will twenty-thousand American dollars suffice?"

"Half that will be more than adequate. I shall report at three. Bonne journée, Madame."

"MONSIEUR DEAN'S BODY WILL BE DELIVERED TO a reputable undertaker in New York within four weeks, and the body preserved until you call for burial. Is that satisfactory, Madame?"

"What name will be used?"

"Madame should not worry herself. I will handle the details here and Mr. Brandeis in New York. Rest assured that when the time comes, you shall be able to bury the girl's father. It is best that I tell you no more."

"Thank you, Mr. Benoit. Here is my bank draft, as promised."

"*Merci.* Will Madame require my services for any other matter?"

"I may. Would you be so kind as to return in one hour?"

"*Très certainement.*"

The next hour proves to be one of the most difficult of my life. That I had lost four loved ones in a matter of months has not prepared me for what I must now do.

"Girls, I have news about your father."

The girls are ecstatic. Ada Mae always the more demonstrative jumps up and down while screaming, "Yes, yes."

Katie, usually less effusive, nonetheless, has difficulty staying still. She grabs Ada Mae, embraces her, and then runs to me and throws her arms around me. Her smile is infectious. Despite what I must tell her, I can't help smiling back at her.

"Quiet, please settle down."

Katie's the first to sit. As she sits, she takes Ada Mae's hand and pulls her down beside her on the bed. Both face me with wide-eyed anticipation. I must begin somewhere. I can't tell the girls their father has been murdered. "There has been an accident. Your father has—"

"Is Father alright? Where is he? When can we see him?" Ada Mae screams.

Katie clutches her arms to her chest as she looks at me with alarm in her eyes. She raises them to ward off what I'm about to say. I believe she knows her father is gone—dead. Leaning as far back into the bed as she can, Katie looks away, face down, as she whispers, "No." Before I speak again, she begins to shake.

"Your father is dead. He was found in the River Seine."

Ada Mae falls back against Katie and buries her head in her sister's lap. Katie raises her head and glares at me.

"No! No, no, no. It's not true. You don't know," she snarls through clenched teeth.

It isn't only the girls who have become dark and sullen. Clouds must have settled below the sun. The room has become dark, a reflection of the mood that has enveloped the girls. It's as if the sadness felt by us has pushed the sun from the room, from our lives. The once colorful duvet has lost its luster; the flowered pattern seems a funeral wreath. We are imprisoned by sadness—grief—depression. I recognize depression and refuse to succumb to its tentacles.

I try to explain what the detective has learned. It does no good. The girls refuse to believe me as they become even more distraught. Gripping one another, sobbing, they try to make sense of what I've told them. I decide not to tell them that he was beaten to death. I'll let them assume he drowned.

Lying on the bed, they eventually—mercifully—cry themselves to sleep. Tucking the girls in, and for the first time, I kiss each one. They don't know; they are asleep. The act of kissing them frees me from doubt. I'll take them to Grisham Manor and make it their new home.

In the morning, they are still upset but talk and listen to what I say. "Do you have any relatives?"

"No, we told you. It was Papa and us. Now it's

just us." Katie remains strong for her sister. Ada Mae's inconsolable in her grief.

Unable to relieve her pain, I begin a difficult conversation. "You will have to make some choices before we leave today."

Katie takes the lead. "What do you mean?"

"The authorities, both the French and the American, don't yet know who your father is, nor about you girls. If we visit your father, the French authorities will take you into custody."

"What does that mean, Miss Lura?"

"It means that they will either turn you over to the American Embassy or place you in a French orphanage until they locate your relatives."

"We already told you we have no relatives."

"I know, Katie."

"How long will we have to stay in an orphanage?"

"When the American authorities learn that you have no relatives, they will return you to America and put you up for adoption."

Katie understands what that means. Ada Mae needs an explanation. "Will we stay together?"

"You might go to different homes." I tell them the truth.

"Can you adopt us?" Katie asks through tears.

Overcome by emotion, I sob and hold my head in my hands. The girls seem to forget their misery. They hold and comfort me.

"I would love to adopt you. But that will be decided in America."

Katie rubs her jaw, looks down, and then up at me. She hesitates for an instant, and says, "Miss Lura, you said we have choices."

I hesitate. I want these two in my life. If I say the wrong thing, I can lose them before I get the chance to earn their love. My Lord, let me earn their love.

"There may be other choices, but there's one I hope you make. I have a lovely home in America that could be your home. We can travel to America. We can bury your father there. He will always be near you." I give them a moment before continuing. "Once we're safe in America and your father has been buried, I could adopt you, keep you together."

There's no whooping or jumping for joy. The girls are spent, but there's love. Both girls come, put their arms around my neck, and kiss my cheeks.

"Thank you," is all I can muster.

MR. BENOIT TELLS ME, "IT IS GOOD THAT MADAME travels without a passport."

"Why?"

"If Madame traveled with a passport, there would be a record of your entry without children. Now you can pass through passport control and claim they are your wards or relatives. You must leave France quickly. If Mr. Dean is identified and the authorities learn two children accompanied him, they will begin a search for them. It will not take La Sûreté long to find you and the girls."

"Can you help me get them out of the country?"

"Madame, the best destination would be America. I can help you get to Le Havre, but you must book a ship. You must leave immediately, today if possible, but in no case later than tomorrow."

"I'll have Claude assist me with booking passage, preferably on *La Touraine*. I'll send a note to you when I have the ship arranged."

Claude arrives after Mr. Benoit takes his leave. "Claude, I must return to America. Would it be possible to book passage through Cook Travel Agency?"

"*Mais bien sur*, Madame. I will be honored to accompany Madame to the agency."

"MADAME, THERE ARE NO FIRST-CLASS ACCOMMO-dations available for the next sailing of *La Touraine*. It is, after all, the height of the season." Money doesn't always fix the problem.

"What about about second class?"

"Of all the second-class cabins, there are but two singles left. We can arrange for two adjoining rooms in third class, but Madame would be most unhappy in such appalling spaces."

"Is there another ship that can accommodate us?" I don't wish to delay our departure any longer than necessary.

"There is another liner leaving two days after *La Touraine*. I'm sure we can arrange for first class."

Unable to wait, I ask, "If I book one of the second-class staterooms, will my nieces have a place to sleep?"

"We can petition the purser to allow the young ladies to sleep on the floor. But Madame would be obliged to provide bedding for them."

"May I book both second-class staterooms?"

"Yes, Madame, but they are located quite far from one another."

I will not have us separated. I book one of the second-class staterooms. Now that I'm experienced with how "small gifts" work, I'm sure that one will guarantee the approval of my petition.

The agency has the booking and the purser's approval completed within the hour. "Madame will board at two tomorrow afternoon. Will Madame require transportation to Le Havre and a hotel near the pier?"

Claude will handle transportation to the railroad station. We have but two hours to return to the hotel, pack, check out, and board the train. I don't have time to reach Mr. Benoit. Claude handles our luggage.

"Madame, once at the hotel, pack what is necessary for tonight, nothing more. I will arrange to have your luggage and bedding for the young ladies delivered to the ship and placed in your stateroom before sailing."

I make a brief stop en route to the hotel. "Claude, please pull to the curb. Girls, wait here with Claude."

Still struggling with the realization that their father's gone forever, they are frightened at the thought of being left alone. Panicked, they grab my arms.

"Don't go," they shout in unison.

"Jeunes dames, Madame Lura will be but a moment. If you check my coat, I'm sure you will find a small amount of the wonderful French Chew." Thank goodness for Claude.

In fewer than five minutes, I return with three purchases, which I conceal in my handbag.

"What did you buy, Miss Lura?" Ada Mae asks.

"It doesn't concern you. We must hurry to the hotel and pack."

"Madame, don't trouble yourself. I will have you at the railroad station in plenty of time."

Claude puts us at ease. My once gruff driver has become a valued friend and guardian.

Delivered to the railway station, I give Claude a warm hug. He seems embarrassed. The girls run into his arms and kiss him. Their show of affection doesn't embarrass him. After giving Claude the money necessary to get our goods delivered to the ship, I offer him a suitable gratuity for all his service. He refuses.

"No, Madame, it is my pleasure to assist. Besides, the agency pays me well."

This is far from the truth. However, there's no arguing with the man. I'll send him a bank draft in care of the agency.

THE GARE SAINT-LAZARE RAILWAY STATION IS where I arrived from Le Havre. The smoke curling from smokestacks of half-a-hundred locomotives had been so dense, it had been almost impossible to see the train on the parallel track, only a few yards away. The sounds, horns, and whistles mixed with the noises of carts and shouts of porters seemed to welcome me to Paris. Exhilaration coursed through me. When I exited the station, a light breeze blew the remaining smoke aside, and I was astonished to see the beauty and grandeur of the sixty-year-old building. I was enthralled by the edifice, the seven-arch entrance, and crowds. Now, fleeing the country, it seems ominous. This time, the horns, whistles, and other sounds seem to shout, "Look—fugitives—stop them." The platforms are crowded with hundreds of people, all strangers, and any could be an agent of La Sûreté, possibly even the people who murdered the girls' father.

As we board the train, I sense danger. Looking up and down the platform, I see nothing amiss amongst the throng of passengers in the gray smoke, but the feeling persists. I'll soon learn that three pairs of eyes were watching.

"Miss Lura, is something wrong?" Katie, always observant, asks.

"No, I'm anxious to begin our trip, our adventure."

"Will Papa be on the train with us?"

"No, that's not possible."

"Will he be on the ship?"

"No, darling. He'll come later, on another ship. I don't know when, maybe in a week or two. When I learn, I will tell you."

The conversation reminds me that I must not forget the agony and fright the two young girls are suffering. It's more than any child should have to endure.

"When will we get to the ship?" Ada Mae asks.

"The train is scheduled to arrive in Le Havre at eight o'clock tonight. The travel agency has arranged for a driver to meet us and take us to a small hotel near the port. It will be late when we get to our rooms. Tomorrow, after lunch, a driver will deliver us to the ship."

"What about our clothes, Miss Lura?" asks Katie.

"Claude has made arrangements to have everything delivered to our stateroom. It should be waiting for us, along with bedding for you to sleep on. It will be an adventure. There is but one single room with a small bed and a tiny bathroom."

An hour before we arrive in Le Havre, the girls fall asleep. I find myself needing to visit the facility and freshen up. Opening the door, two men block my exit. Even before I see their faces, I know who they are. I recognize their smell—fish, urine, and stale wine. They are the same two hoodlums who accosted me at the Louvre and followed us. "Let me pass."

The taller of the two speaks in heavily accented English. "We will have Madame's necklace."

"No. You shall not," I protest, holding tight to my pendant. Is this what they have been after all this time?

The girls wake. I can hear them sobbing. "You've frightened my girls. Leave us alone. Go away."

The shorter man pulls a wicked-looking dagger from under his coat. "Give us what we want, or I will give you a taste of this."

I hear a voice from behind the ruffians. "That's a gun in your back. Drop the knife, or I'll shoot you where you stand." The knife falls from the man's hand.

"Madame, please close the door. Don't open it again until the train reaches Le Havre."

The two ruffians seem to fall back. As I close the door, I recognize the now-familiar shape of the light-haired man with a bowler and dark overcoat pulling the two back into the shadows.

The stranger has come to our rescue once again. Who is he? What can he want?

I'm as frightened as the girls.

"I have to pee," Ada Mae announces, followed by Katie's, "Me too."

"You must wait. It isn't safe to leave the compartment." I'm probably more in need of the facility than either of the girls. We huddle in uncomfortable silence until the train comes to a halt. Afraid of what might await us in the corridor, I hesitate to open the door.

Once most of the passengers have left the train, there's a knock at the door. When I ask who is there, a clear voice announces that he is the conductor and that we must leave the train.

Looking out the window, we see people— passengers—hurrying in all directions. I open the door, cautiously. Other than an elderly gentleman in a conductor's uniform, the only other people I see appear to be passengers hurrying to get off the train. After a quick dash to the facility, we rush to leave the train.

Once we are inside the Le Havre station, I hear a page calling my name, "Madame Myer." He has a telegram from Claude. It states, "Please go with the page. He will take you to your cab."

Safely ensconced at the small hotel Claude arranged for us, I relax enough to doze, although my sleep is haunted by dreams of the ruffians who have threatened us. After a restless night, we wake to a beautiful June day. The proprietress is friendly and gregarious. As she serves us a breakfast of omelets, fruit, pastries, and strong coffee in the minuscule dining room, her running commentary never ceases. I find one bit of news interesting.

"When I went for eggs and baguettes this morning, the baker, who provides the passenger train with bread, told me the conductor told him an interesting story." Without waiting to see if we are interested, she continues, "It seems that once all the passengers were off the train, the cleaners found two men locked in an empty compartment." She walks out of the room, still speaking, and the girls and I look at each other. Katie starts to say something, but I put a hand up to shush her as our hostess returns. She takes up right where she left off.

"Both men were unconscious, but that wasn't all. When the Gendarmes took them away, they found the men's hands broken. It looked as if someone beat them with a club or a hammer. When interrogated, they refused to answer questions."

We hurry through breakfast and return to our room. The girls speak in unison. "Miss Lura, do you think those are the men who frightened us?"

I'm not sure I want to know if they are the same men or not. "I don't know. Shall we bathe? I want to go shopping before we go to the ship." I've said the magic word, shopping.

Katie's excited about the prospect of shopping, while Ada Mae wants to get a coat to wear on the ship. "The ship was ever so cold on the trip here. I don't want to get cold this time."

Katie decides that we need to get "A big bag of French Chew."

The girls forget all about the thugs as they talk of what they would like to get before we go aboard the ship.

EIGHTEEN

SECOND-CLASS PASSENGERS BOARD HERE

The sign, painted in bold black print, is less about direction than class distinction.

At the docks early, we find a group has already formed a line at the foot of the gangway to the *La Touraine*. As the girls and I join the others waiting in line, I'm sure this will be the first of many differences to come.

We queue up and make our way to the foot of the gangway where an immigration official waits with a clipboard.

"Your boarding pass and travel documents." I hand him the boarding passes for the girls and myself.

"What about these girls? Who are they? They don't share your last name."

"My nieces."

"I don't have all day. You must show me

something that allows them to be in your company."

Mr. Benoit had told me I might run into this problem, and he had provided an answer. I hand the man an unsealed envelope. He examines the contents—two-hundred francs.

"This will suffice."

At the top of the gangway, a purser waits. After a glance at our boarding passes, he says, "Through the door to the second passageway and turn right. Your cabin is on the left." He dismisses us with a vague nod in the direction of the door.

The difference in the treatment I experienced a few weeks earlier on this very same ship as a first-class passenger is striking. There had been no line, no waiting, and I had been escorted from the dock to my stateroom.

Claude's promise to have our luggage delivered was a godsend. However, delivery is all he managed to arrange. Unlike the butler and maid I was provided in first class, there's no such service in second class. Our luggage is lying on the floor. That wouldn't have been a problem, except there's no room left for us to move about the cabin. If the accommodations are this poor in second class, I can't imagine what the poor souls in third class must endure.

"This is not like my stateroom on the way here." I immediately regret saying it as the girls bombard me with questions.

"What do you mean?"

"Well, if you must know—"

"You must tell us," Katie demands.

"Alright, alright. When I traveled from New York to Le Havre, I was in first class. The facility was as large as this entire cabin."

Ada Mae interrupts with, "What's a facility?'

"The bathroom."

"What was the bed like?"

"The bed was big enough for three people. It had a canopy and was as soft as sleeping on a cloud."

I can't help laughing as I pull the girls down onto a lumpy bed, hardly large enough for one person.

"There was a vanity with three mirrors, a reading table with two chairs and an armoire—that's a large cabinet—for my clothes."

I'm disappointed but manage a smile for the girls' sake. They take it all in stride, and we soon have everything stowed as best we can. An inside cabin, there's no porthole or balcony. The bed, as small as it is, is large enough for both girls. I let them share it.

"I'll sleep on the floor."

"No, Miss Lura. Ada Mae and I'll sleep on the floor. It's part of the adventure. Papa let us do it when we came to France."

The dinner hour is nearing as we finish settling in. The bathroom will be a challenge for the three of us. I must ring for the maid to bring more towels. I search the room but find no means to summon anyone.

"Girls, I'm going to find the maid. Do you want to wait here or go with me?"

Both jump at the opportunity and are out the door before I can get my hat and shawl. The second-class area is small, with no direct access to the forward part of the ship. Both first and third-class passengers have a promenade that circles the vessel. We have two short walking areas, one on either side of the ship.

"How may we find a maid?" I ask a crewmember who is cleaning windows.

"I'm sorry, ma'am. There are no maids in second class, only room attendants. They come around in the morning and again after supper."

This is not acceptable, but it isn't the man's fault.

"Kindly direct me to the purser's office."

"Second -class passengers are not allowed on the first-class decks. That's where he's located. There's an assistant purser for second class. His office is open from ten to four. He won't be back until tomorrow morning."

"What about meals? Where's the second-class dining room?"

"Your dining room is down one flight of stairs. Dinner is served from six until eight." Looking at his watch, he says, "Service starts in fifteen minutes."

Tired from the train ride from Paris to Le Havre, we decide to eat at six, so we may get to bed early.

In the dining room, I find yet more differences in service. There are no escorts to take us to an assigned table; we sit anywhere we please. Waiters do bring our dinner. Instead of the extensive menu I enjoyed in first class, there are soups, salads, and choice of two dishes. I choose the fish. The girls both ask for the pork chops.

Katie has trouble with her chop. When I ask if she needs help, Ada Mae pipes up. "She doesn't know how to cut her food. Papa always did it for her."

At the mention of their father, both girls begin to sniffle, and Katie drops her knife and fork.

"There, there, let me help you." I cut her chop and vegetables into bitesize pieces. Putting the knife and fork down on her plate, I use my handkerchief to wipe the tears from her eyes. Turning to Ada Mae, I see she has stopped sniffling and has finished cutting her chop. Her vegetables are shoved as far away from the meat as the plate will allow.

The fish is excellent. I don't believe I had better in first class. There is nothing unwholesome about the meal. The girls fuss over their vegetables, but they are just being children.

Hurrying back to the cabin, we find an attendant leaving.

"Good evening. This is our cabin. Please be so kind as to provide us with two more sets of towels."

"I'm sorry, ma'am, but we are not allowed to do that."

I'm upset but don't show it. In first class, there was always an abundance of towels and toiletries. Once again, I think of Mr. Benoit's small gifts. I invite her back into the cabin where one-hundred francs gets two sets of towels, and we come to an understanding. I'll leave an envelope with one-hundred francs for her each day. In return, we'll have our cabin cleaned as necessary, the bed made up, and the towels always fresh. If I'm pleased with her service, the last day the envelope will contain five-hundred francs.

"If I need additional service, how will I reach you?"

"Stop any of the crew, but none of the officers, and ask to have me notified. My name is Colette. I will come to your cabin as soon as I can."

After she leaves, we prepare for bed, which is an adventure of its own. I turn the tiny bed down and use the bathroom. Finished, I exit the cramped facility, stepping carefully over the already sleeping Ada Mae. The floor isn't visible except under the desk that also serves as our vanity, sans mirror.

"Miss Lura, this will be a fun adventure."

"Katie, we don't want to wake Ada Mae. Please talk softly. Now we must rest. I can sleep with Ada Mae if you wish."

"No, ma'am. She'll cry if she wakes up and I'm not here."

OUR FIRST NIGHT AT SEA IS ROUGH. AS WE CLEAR the coast, the onshore rollers are noticeable, and I have difficulty sleeping. When I finally do, it seems only moments before Katie wakes me.

"Miss Lura, Ada Mae's sick. She got sick the first

night on the ship from America too."

The foul odor of vomit fills the room. Calling Colette will do no good. Ada Mae's bent over the toilet. Good. Any more will go in there. There's a puddle on the girls' bedding and a stream to the tiny bathroom. This is one time I'm happy the bathroom is so close. Picking up the soiled linen, I roll up the sheets and dump the mess outside the cabin door. I hope this will be the only set I'm forced to set out.

"Are you feeling better?" Katie asks her sister but doesn't allow her time to answer.

"I don't think she'll throw up anymore, but she has some of it on her nightie. If you give me another, I'll help her."

I hand Katie a clean one, and the girls crowd into the bathroom and close the door. They prefer to dress out of my sight. I'm not sure if it's plain old-fashioned modesty, or if they are uncomfortable around me. Am I still a stranger to them? I'm about to doze off when they reappear, all smiles and giggles.

"Girls." They freeze. "Get in the bed. I'll sleep on the floor." Both attempt to protest, but I will hear none of it.

"Do it and be still." Surprised by the tone of my voice, they hush and settle down on the small bed, where they are asleep within minutes.

I find myself tossing and turning, and not from the motion of the ship. Awakening at six, I'm nauseous, bile rising in my throat. I dart to the facility and manage to reach the commode before losing what remains of my dinner. Thank goodness, the girls were on the bed and not asleep on the floor blocking the door. I manage another hour of fitful sleep before I wake to find them dressed and ready for breakfast. Eager to eat, they hurry me along. We reach the dining room moments before serving is finished.

Egg dishes have already been discontinued, but *crêpes*—it is a French ship after all—are available. The girls call them skinny pancakes. At first, they make faces because they want maple syrup, and there's none, but it only lasts seconds. The crepes, served with strawberry preserves and whipped cream, are a treat. Ada Mae enjoys them so much, I scold her for the uncouth way she tries to fork half a crepe into her mouth with each bite. It appears she has already forgotten how she vomited her last meal.

Finished with breakfast, we return to our cabin to freshen up before deciding how we shall spend the rest of the morning. As we turn down the passageway leading from the dining room, I notice a tall man with light brown hair. Catching his eye, he freezes for a moment before abruptly turning and walking hurriedly to the next corner. There's something familiar about him—his eyes maybe—I can't quite put my finger on it. When we enter the passageway, he has disappeared. What is it about this man? The question troubles me all the way back to our cabin.

"WE MUST NOT NEGLECT YOUR STUDIES." I BOUGHT books for them when we stopped at the bookstore in Paris. "We shall read for an hour every day and then work on reckoning for another hour."

"Miss Lura, why must I read and do numbers?" Ada Mae is reluctant.

"Ladies need an education in a world dominated by men. Until our education is equal to theirs, it will be difficult—no, impossible—for women to take their rightful place in society."

I doubt they understand me, but no matter, we begin.

"Ada Mae, for you, I have Mr. Lewis Carroll's book that he wrote about a young lady like you."

"Oh, who's that?" A frown accompanies her question.

"Her name's Alice, and the book is called *Alice's Adventures in Wonderland*. You will adore it." More feminine and imaginative than her sister, I'm sure this is the right book for her.

"What about me?" Katie quips.

"For you, I have *Treasure Island*. It's about the adventures of a young boy, Jim Hawkins. He falls in with pirates searching for buried treasure. A Scotsman, Robert Louis Stevenson, wrote it." I'm sure Katie, somewhat of a tomboy and the more adventurous of the two, will find it to her liking.

Handing each their book, I say, "I'll read mine while you read yours. If you have any questions or need help with words, ask me. When we finish reading ours, we can trade." Handing might not be the right term as Katie snatches hers from my hand. Ada Mae places her hands under her behind and adopts an indifferent posture.

"Ada Mae."

Her frown deepens in response. My response is to place the unwanted book on her lap.

"What are you reading, Miss Lura?" Katie asks.

"*The Adventures of Sherlock Holmes.*"

"Who's he?"

"Mr. Holmes is an English detective. Another Englishman, Arthur Conan Doyle, created his character. The book is a collection of short stories telling of his adventures in London, England. So, we're all reading adventure stories. Now let's get comfortable and get started."

"Oh, alright. But can we at least go on deck and read in the sun?" a still angry Ada Mae, retorts.

I agree to her demand. It's a small price to pay to get her to accept my mandate. Getting their cooperation, especially hers, is going to be more difficult than I imagined. Was I this pigheaded at her age? I can't help smiling at my next thought. Probably.

An hour later, Ada Mae's at the limits of her patience. She remains in her deckchair, but her head is tilted back as she gazes skyward. I can't ignore the noise she makes tapping her foot on the floor.

"Ada Mae, are you alright?"

"I'm tired of reading. I want to do something else."

"Don't you enjoy Alice?"

"Oh, yes, but I'm tired of reading."

I tell her she can put her book away. Katie looks up at me. "Do I have to stop? Please, I want to keep reading."

"Certainly. I'll never stop you from reading."

Ada Mae's continued fidgeting distracts both Katie and me. Taking her by the hand, we walk to the rail. I feel her squeeze, holding tight to me. I look down as she looks up and smiles. Is she acting, or has she gotten over our squabble? I pray it's the latter and smile back at her.

If she's acting, it's an excellent job. Her temper tantrum was wearing on me, and for the briefest instant, the outburst made me question my desire to make the girls a permanent part of my life.

It's a stunning sunlit day, not a cloud in sight, the beauty of the cobalt sea melts into the deep blue of the sky. The only thing in sight is a large sea turtle floating on the surface.

The peaceful setting is shattered by a loud blast from the ship's horn. Two more follow in quick succession. Startled, I pull Ada Mae close and start toward Katie, who sits up, still holding her book. She doesn't move, as though frozen—rooted in place— eyes wide with fear.

Once I have both girls, I look around. We're not the only ones frightened by this sudden blowing of the horns. Not one passenger remains seated; all have come to their feet with most standing at the rails, like me, looking for any sign of danger.

Other than the sea turtle, there's nothing visible on the ocean's surface to the horizon. And as far as I can tell, the ship has not suffered any malady. Looking around for a source of concern, I spot Colette carrying an armload of linens. We hurry to her side, where Katie pleas for an answer to the startling event.

Colette can see that the girls are frightened by the way they cling to me as their heads swivel about. I'm relieved when she kneels and faces the girls with a reassuring smile.

"There is nothing to fear."

Comforted by her calm and friendly demeanor, Ada Mae and I relax. Katie continues to hold me in a solid grip as she flinches at every sound. I do something I've not done before, I pick her up and hold her tightly. Her head on my shoulder, I can hear quiet whimpering.

Rocking her gently, I tell Colette to explain in hopes her story will help calm Katie.

"The captain normally makes an announcement the day before we arrive at this location. I can't understand why he failed to do so, Madame."

"Tell us. Tell us," demands the no longer frightened Ada Mae, bouncing from foot to foot.

"When we pass this position, all French vessels sound the ship's horn in honor of a great battle fought here ninety years ago." Colette looks over her shoulder and lowers her voice. "I can't stand around talking. I have duties. I'm sorry."

"I may have a solution," I whisper.

"Excuse me," I announce in a voice loud and haughty so that other passengers and members of the staff can hear me. "I require your assistance, Mademoiselle. Would you be so kind as to accompany us to our cabin?"

Biting her lip to stifle a smile, Collette opens and holds the door for us to enter the passageway. Once in our stateroom, she continues the story.

"As I said, ninety years ago, there was a great sea battle. It was between the British ship, HMS *George*, and France's *Marine Nationale*, *Marseille*. The British fleet had blockaded the French coast all along the Bay of Biscay. The French admiral ordered the larger warships under his command to break the blockade. The warship *Marseille* made a heroic attempt to break free. Near this exact spot, she encountered the HMS *George*."

"She?" Katie asks.

"Yes, she. Just as *La Touraine* is called she, all ships, including the HMS *George*, are called she."

"But George is a man's name."

"It's tradition. Ships are called she. Don't ask me why. I must hurry. I can't stay long."

"Oh, please, go on."

"HMS *George* was armed with seventy-four cannons—they were called guns—*Marseille* with eighty. The battle began in the late afternoon and continued throughout the night. At dawn, the two ships came together. It is said, they were side-by-side, no more than two meters apart, when forty French and over thirty British cannons fired devastating salvos. Both ships were mortally wounded and sank within minutes. Nearly eight-hundred men went to the bottom of the sea; six survived, three French and an equal number of British. None of the French spoke English, and the British sailors didn't speak French."

"How'd they stay alive?" Katie asks.

"One of the hatch covers floated free of the *Marseille,* and all six men clung to it."

"What happened to them?"

"After two days, they were spotted by a British man-of-war. The French sailors were held captive as prisoners of war in England for the duration of the conflict. The British seamen joined the crew of the ship that rescued them. I have been away from my duties far too long. I must go."

"But, why did the ship blow its horns?"

"To honor the memory of the brave French and British sailors who died fighting for their countries."

NINETEEN

THE THIRD DAY AT SEA, I LEAVE THE GIRLS TO NAP
while I walk, *Sherlock,* under my arm. Almost to the
end of the second-class promenade, I spy the blond
man fast asleep on a deckchair covered with a light
blanket. A dark topcoat rests on the chair to his right.
Despite a full beard, he seems so familiar. It's time
that I find out who this strange man is and why he
seems so familiar.

The deck is busy with passengers, so I stop at the
rail a discreet distance away and watch for movement.
I don't wish to be too conspicuous, but the man is
unmoving. I tire and take a deckchair near him,
*Sherloc*k open to some unknown page. He appears to
be fast asleep, and I take the opportunity to move
closer to get a clear view of his face. Standing, I move
deliberately to the chair closest to him. No one pays
me any mind. I sit and peek at his face. Even covered

by a beard, the line of his chin seems familiar. As I try to get a better look, he burrows down into his blanket in slumber, snoring once.

I decide I'm done with all this hiding and sneaking about. Lifting *Sherlock* above my head, I look around—no one is watching—and drop the book on the deck.

The blond man opens his eyes and gapes, looks away, blinks, and stares wide-eyed.

"Ah. . ." he mumbles, "ah, excuse me. . ." and retrieves his topcoat uncovering a bowler.

"It's you."

He gets to his feet in a feeble attempt to flee. I bar his way and move closer until we are mere inches apart, face to face. His eyes, green with flecks of gold reflected in the bright sunlight, trap my gaze. I know those eyes.

"Who are you?"

The man falls back on the deckchair with an audible sigh. His gaze darts about, as if in search of an escape route.

"Why have you been following me?"

He looks as though he would rather be anywhere else than here.

"You have me at a disadvantage, madam."

He stands up, all official-like, puts on his bowler, drapes the topcoat over his shoulders, possibly thinking the mere performance of getting ready to leave will make me back down. I move closer, hugging *Sherlock* to my chest.

"Please, excuse me," he mumbles. "I must return to my cabin."

"You're not going anywhere. If you insist on leaving, I will scream. Do you understand?"

"Allow me a moment, and I shall explain all."

"I should hope so. You've been following me for quite some time."

He gives a small shrug as his shoulders fall. After a few deep breaths, he says, "My name is Joseph Myer."

I've seen that glance, the same eyes, same gait, same cowlick in the sideburn—he is a Myer. I can't help but step back, my heart banging hard, the pulse pounding in my ears. I know it before the man speaks.

"I'm Walter's half-brother." He hesitates, then adds, "Illegitimate if you will."

Recoiling, dazed, it is I who is taken aback. My breath fails me, and overcome by weakness, I slump and almost fall on to the deckchair. My God, his voice, he sounds like Walter.

"Are you ill? Should I call for a doctor?"

"I'll be fine. The ship rocked and put me off balance."

"Well, that's good," he says.

"He never mentioned you." But I know. There is no doubt in my mind, with those eyes, he could only be a Myer.

"He didn't know about me. Our father was a major in the Union Army. In November 1863, he was wounded at Chattanooga. Mother was a nurse at the military hospital where he was treated and recuperated. They fell in love, and I was born in 1864."

"But he was married. What of his wife? Did she know?"

"Mrs. Myer never knew. I don't think the Major did either. My mother never saw him again after he was discharged from the hospital."

How should I respond to him? Respond? Overcome with nausea and a feeling of lightheadedness, I don't want to believe Walter's father could have done such a thing.

"Why should I believe you?"

"My mother's dead. Walter's dead. You're the one living relative I have, and that's tenuous at best."

His breath is labored, he sinks lower, and even though no tears fall, his eyes are watery.

"Mrs. Myer, there's no reason for you to believe me. If you choose not to, that will be your decision."

I don't wish to believe him, but it's obvious. He has the same gold-flecked green eyes, the same voice, the same physique as Walter. This man is a Myer.

"Why have you been following me?"

"Before my mother died—it's been two years— she gave me this picture."

He hands me a faded photograph. It's grainy and time-worn, but there's no question the uniformed man is Joseph Myer, Walter's father.

"When she told me about Major Myer, she also

told me that she named me after him. Until she gave me this picture, she refused to tell me who my father was, saying that he died in the war. After she passed away, I hired detectives to find him. I learned he had died, and I had a half-brother named Walter. When I heard of the death of your parents, I decided to reach out to Walter when the two of you came to New York."

"Why New York? Why not at our home in Ridgefield?"

"My practice is in New York. I thought it would be better there. I didn't want to surprise him unannounced in Ridgefield. What if the meeting went badly?"

"Practice? Are you a doctor?"

"No, an attorney."

Checking my watch, I realize I've been gone for well over an hour.

"Mr. Myer, I'm inclined to believe you. I need to return to my girls. They will wonder what has become of me. Would you care to join us at dinner? We can talk further."

"I'd be honored. What will you tell the girls?"

"The truth, to a point."

"Excuse me," says an overdressed woman.

She must have startled Mr. Myer because his hands clench into fists before he sighs and nods in her direction.

"Yes?"

"I'm a first-class passenger, and somehow, I

found myself here. Can you direct me to the first-class deck or to someone capable of showing me the way?"

His annoyance is visible. "I'd be more than happy to tell you where you belong." The woman is oblivious to his feigned desire to assist her.

Before he can say more, a crewman approaches, and I ask him to assist the woman back to first class.

"My, but you were more than a little unpleasant to that poor woman."

"She caught me off guard. Besides, I detest people who think they are better than the rest of us." After he takes a deep breath and exhales, he adds, "But you're right. My behavior was inexcusable."

"Before we meet for dinner, I'll tell the girls you're my husband's long-lost brother and that we met today by happenstance. Is that satisfactory?"

"Quite. I'm happy to meet you, Mrs. Myer, finally. I'll call for you at six."

RETURNING TO THE CABIN, I TELL THE GIRLS I HAVE some exciting news. Both tilt their heads and look at me with wide eyes.

"I met someone related to me."

"Who?" Ada Mae asks.

"My husband's brother, Joseph Myer."

She starts to speak again when Katie shushes her. "Quiet Ada Mae."

"But—"

THE MONA LISA SISTERS

"I said, be quiet." She gives me a questioning look and begins to tap her teeth with her right forefinger. She squints and says, "What's he doing on the ship? Do you know him?"

"It's a long story, one I will tell you later. All I can tell you now is that you will meet him at dinner."

"What does he look like? Is he handsome? Is he old?" Ada Mae takes her turn.

Her questions take me by surprise. "You can see for yourself when you meet him. Now I have an errand to run."

Telling the girls to work on either their reading or numbers—they do not need to know the nature of my task—I hurry off to the Assistant Purser's Office. I arrive minutes before he closes.

"I wish to send a telegram."

I send a request to Attorney Brandeis asking him to investigate Joseph Myer, an attorney, Walter's brother.

THE NOVELTY OF MEETING A STRANGER WEARS OFF as we dress for dinner. Katie is soon deeply engrossed in her book. Never one to spend a great deal of effort on my makeup, I'm taken by surprise when Ada Mae asks if she can use one of my lipsticks to "Paint my lips."

"No. You are much too young to even think about using makeup."

From the look on her face, I'm sure I can expect

an episode of her pouting. I'm pleasantly surprised when her face transforms into a smile, and she returns to her arithmetic reckoning.

Promptly at six, there's a knock at the door. Rushing to answer, the girls crash into each other and almost fall over one another. Recovering first, Ada Mae pulls the door open with a flourish. Katie curtsies behind her, not even looking up.

"Why, good evening ladies." Mr. Myer bows and proclaims, "It's a pleasure to meet you. My name's Joseph Myer. Please call me Joseph."

"Good evening. I'm Ada Mae Dean, and this is my sister Katie." She curtsies. "Please come in. We've been expecting you."

I smile at Ada Mae's formal tone. Joseph obliges her with a flourish of his own, a deep bow with his bowler at his chest. Katie, though reticent, finally braves a look upward and immediately says, "You're the man from the train," her hand pointed at him.

Mr. Myer looks to me for direction, but I'm a little lost. I didn't know she could be that perceptive.

"It's a long story. If Mrs. Myer agrees, I'll wait to explain until after we get to know one another a little better."

"I approve," I say, embracing the girls' shoulders. "I'm famished. I don't know about you."

"We can eat, too," says Ada Mae.

"But of course," Joseph says and opens the cabin door. He bows with another theatrical flourish and announces, "This way, my ladies."

Once we are seated at a table for four, Joseph suggests we order before we go on with introductions. I select the fresh sea bass. The girls inform the waiter that they will wait until after Joseph has placed his order. He promptly makes a show of indecision as he holds the menu up, hiding his face from the girls. He winks at me then makes a ridiculous spectacle ordering the other entrée on the menu, pot roast with steamed carrots and brussels sprouts.

"I'll have the same," the girls say in unison.

"Except for the brussels sprouts," adds Ada Mae.

"Bring the sprouts," I say and turn to Ada Mae. "You will eat your vegetables."

She starts to object, but the look I give her stops all thought of dispute.

"Miss Lura says that you're her husband's brother, but you didn't know him," says Katie.

"Yes, ma'am."

"You never played with him?"

Mr. Myer looks first to Ada Mae and then Katie.

"No. Last year, I learned I had a brother. We never met. But I found out he was an engineer and that he built railroad bridges."

Our salads arrive, looking wilted by the lack of water and sun-scorched. I give the waiter an inquiring look, his response, an apologetic shrug.

"*Je suis désolé Madame.* It is impossible to . . . how you say . . . fresh . . . keep les legumes, the vegetables fresh."

"Je comprends, monsieur."

Facing his salad, Joseph twists his mouth in amusement. The girls giggle. He takes a bite, and they follow suit.

"What do you do?" asks Ada Mae.

"I'm a lawyer. I live and work in New York. Do you know where New York is?"

"Of course, we know where New York is," Ada Mae says, exasperated. "We live in Boston with our papa."

At the mention of their father, both girls fall silent. Ada Mae bends forward, hands tightly clenched. She pulls her fists to her chest. If her fingers were intertwined, she would almost appear to be in prayer.

Katie stands, buries her face in my hair, sobbing. Wrapping my arms around her helps me control my emotions.

When Ada Mae looks up, I free an arm and beckon for her to come to me. She looks down and, after a few seconds, also comes to me.

Joseph looks aghast and turns to me, palms up, eyes wide. Have I caused this? his face asks. He has no idea what's happening.

I shake my head.

After a few minutes, the girls have recovered enough to return to their seats. Dessert is strawberry shortcake with ice cream, but the girls barely look at it, their eyes locked on Mr. Myer.

"Why didn't you write to your brother?" Ada

Mae asks. "If I found out I had a sister somewhere, other than Katie, I would send her a letter."

"Me too," chimes in Katie.

"I wanted to wait until Walter and Miss Lura came to New York to introduce myself. I knew they lived in Connecticut but that they would come to New York for business. I guess I waited too long."

My smile dies, and I feel like I'm at the bottom of the well when Katie asks. "What do you mean?"

"The last time they came to New York was when they came for the birth of their child. There was a terrible accident. My brother, Walter, was killed, and Miss Lura lost the baby."

The girls turn to me, mouths agape. They make no sound—tears stream down their faces.

"What's wrong with you? Have you no concern?"

He is instantly on his feet—crestfallen—mortified.

Rising, I pull the girls closer, about to whisk them away.

"I'm sorry," he pleads. "How could I have known they didn't know."

The diners at the surrounding tables stare, their faces congealed in surprise.

"We can continue this conversation tomorrow." This is not a scene I want prolonged.

I rush with the girls back to our cabin, leaving Joseph in bewildered embarrassment. I feel foolish for letting him into my life so easily.

For the girls' sake, I force myself into a semblance of control and let them cry it out. They cry for their father. Deep within the core of my soul, I cry for my loss. The girls' tears are without shame for the pain that must all but devour them. The same powerful, debilitating grief that consumed and exhausted me for those many months of terrible despair. I don't know how long they cry, but I awake after midnight to find the three of us on the tiny bed. Covering them, I lie on the floor in my dress, where my tears return.

I wake to a brutal throbbing in my head. An hour of sleep, maybe two? I peer at the clock and realize we have already missed breakfast. Forcing myself up, it takes me a moment to find my balance. The girls are up. Ada Mae's bathed and dressed. Katie's still in her nightgown, under the lamp, reading. Caught off guard, she slams her book shut.

"Katie?"

"Jim Hawkins is in—"

"I'm sure young Master Hawkins can wait until you're dressed for the day."

She stomps into the bathroom, murmuring under her breath. Ada Mae seems to relish the fact that she's not the one in trouble. She smiles angelically at me and brushes her hair.

Without a porthole to check, I assume the summer weather will be pleasant and opt for a light frock. But once on deck, we find the day is overcast and cold. We return to the cabin and change into warmer clothes. Back out on the promenade, Joseph's the first person we see, and not by chance, I'm sure. There's a liveliness in the way he steps up to us while avoiding my eyes and focusing on the girls.

"Good morning, ladies," he says while executing a dramatic bow. The girls giggle.

"I hope you slept well."

"We slept like pirates," Katie announces, and Joseph steps back in mock surprise.

He switches his attention to Ada Mae and bows again.

I can't help but smile. It's amazing how the girls have taken such an immediate liking to him. Poor things miss their father. Their enthusiasm seems to melt away any lingering reservations I might have harbored about him. He smiles. His ability to change sorrow into lightheartedness after such a night is amazing.

"Since we are family, you may as well call me Lura."

Two men farther down the promenade get into a shouting match that escalates into shoving. I instinctively gather the girls around me, trying to cover their ears. Any mirth we had is sucked out of our idyllic interlude and my heart races. Joseph's also startled, but by the time he turns in the direction of the ruckus, the skirmish proves to be less serious than it first appeared. The antagonists embrace drunkenly and go on their merry way.

"Look, look," Ada Mae screams, running to the railing and pointing.

Pulled from thoughts of thugs, I look to where she points. I see fish, dozens of them, gliding above and across the water. They appear birdlike. I've heard of these creatures, Flying Fish, but this is the first time I've seen any.

Smiling broadly, Joseph winks at me, catching me off guard. He doesn't seem to notice, and a pleasantly warm sensation replaces my surprise.

"Girls, those are Flying Fish," he says. "They roam the world in warm waters but are less common here in the North Atlantic. I first saw them on a trip to China."

"Why do they fly?"

"It's believed they developed the skill to avoid being eaten by bigger fish. When you see this many, you can expect to see a school of larger fish following along behind. If you look closely, you can see large dark shadows below them."

I see several rapidly moving shapes below the surface and point them out.

"They can, on occasion, stay in the air for a distance as long as the length of this ship."

Ada Mae's curious and asks how high they can fly.

Looking over her, I see that Joseph is watching me. I return the look, holding his gaze.

After a few seconds, he blinks away.

"Well, Mr. Myer, what do you think? Are you

excited?" I blush; he blushes.

"What?"

"By the fish?"

"Miss Lura, how high can they go?"

"I should imagine Joseph can answer that better than I."

"How high would you like them to go, Mrs. Myer?"

It isn't long before the novelty wears off, and the girls are ready to continue our walk. Glancing at Joseph, I'm not sure he is.

Walking in a comfortable silence twice more around the deck on his arm, I find myself sneaking furtive glances at him. Several times, I catch him doing the same toward me until Katie announces, "I'm hungry."

"We missed breakfast, and if I don't have something to eat, I will shrivel up and blow away," chimes in Ada Mae.

"I would like to see that young lady, but I'm also hungry." I invite Joseph to join us.

"Of course. Allow me to lead the way?"

"You never told us how high," Ada Mae demands for the third or fourth time.

I laugh. Joseph seems flustered.

"The Flying Fish. Remember, you're the expert."

"I'm not an expert, Ada Mae. But we are safe up here on the ship. It might be different if we were in a small open boat."

Having missed breakfast, the girls and I are

ravenous. I manage to eat my soup and salad in a manner befitting a lady. The girls have no such reservations about appearing ladylike. My attempts to slow them down fail. Joseph doesn't seem to mind their unseemly behavior in the least. He merely smiles.

Turning his attention from the girls to me, Joseph's smile widens. "You look particularly lovely today," he says. The girls snicker, and his face reddens.

"I feel lovely, Mr. Myer."

My friendly retort seems to reduce his embarrassment as his face loses its reddish tint and returns to an attractive tan. Our conversation continues in this vein for several minutes. If I didn't know better, I would say our tête-à-tête borders on flirtation. Whatever has happened to me? I'm still officially in mourning for Walter.

Lunch finished, I ask Joseph to excuse us as I want to rest and ponder my decision to adopt the girls. I tell him the girls have their studies waiting.

RETURNING TO THE STATEROOM, I FIND A TELEGRAM slipped under the door.

Mrs. Lura Myer
Joseph Myer first-rate lawyer Stop Known Personally Stop. Story about mother true Stop. Bartolini will meet ship Stop Further requests?
Brandeis

I can't explain why this news makes me happy, but it does. Eyes closed, pleased, I have the strangest sensation that destiny has taken a hand in bringing the four of us together. I want to talk to Joseph, see him, but without it appearing so. I tell the girls I shall take a turn around the promenade while they complete their studies. They promise they will, and I leave with my promise to return within an hour.

On my second circuit, I pause at the deckchair where I first saw him. Him? Joseph. Maybe he'll return for another snooze. I'm struck by the idea that a short nap might be pleasant and relax on the adjoining chair. A crew member stops and offers me a blanket. For some reason, I'm embarrassed and decline. As soon as he moves on, I rise and continue my stroll.

Why haven't I seen him? Since I found him here, asleep, he has been on deck every time I've come out here. There's a sudden chill in the air, and I go back inside. As I pass the salon, I see Joseph enjoying a cigar. I stop and wait until he glances up and notices me. I smile and continue my stroll—slowly. I want to give him the opportunity to catch up if he wishes.

Before I reach the passage back to the deck, he's at my side.

"Please, may I walk with you?"

I agree.

Before we walk on, he asks my pardon before he uses an ornately engraved silver cigar cutter to remove the lit end of his cigar. He places the remainder in an equally opulent case. I'm enthralled with the design. He offers his arm, and I take it as we make our way to the promenade. This time of day, it's very popular, but we find an area where we sit and talk with a measure of privacy.

"That bamboo design on your cigar case is quite beautiful."

"Look at the dragon," Joseph says and turns it over.

The dragon is even more amazing than the bamboo. Winged and with flames issuing from a fanged mouth, it appears to be in flight. The eyes are a deep red ruby with a hint of blue.

"Where did you get such a magnificent case?"

"Last year, I traveled with clients, members of the Wheat Growers Association, to China on business. Our flour industries are competing with the Chinese for a larger share of the world market." Handing me the case, he adds, "It was a gift from our Chinese hosts."

"That is interesting. Do you have any idea of the extent of the Chinese rail systems?"

"Somewhat."

When I see Louis Brandeis and Giovanni, I must have them look at wheat and the orient for potential investment opportunities.

"Thank you for breaking away from your cigar."

"My pleasure."

"I would like to know more about the Chinese markets and the flour industry." This could be an interesting conversation—ostensibly business curiosity—allowing me to observe Joseph and learn the depth of his business acumen and knowledge of world trade.

Joseph explains the two issues from both a business and legal standpoint. He has an excellent understanding of each. Even more impressive is the way he converses with me. Unlike most men of his standing, he doesn't talk down to me—a woman. Our discussion is open, frank, between equals. In this regard, he once again reminds me of Walter. I realize I can trust him with my life. Could I—would I— trust him with my heart?

"I must return to the girls and only have a few minutes, but I have a request. I'll have you know that Mr. Louis Brandeis represents my business interests and that when we first spoke, I sent him a telegram."

Joseph smiles, "I know Louis."

"So, I understand. I want to retain you for a personal matter."

"I'm listening," he says with a grin, "but I must warn you, I'm expensive."

"And I'm very wealthy." Our talk about the orient and the flour industry has convinced me that he is more than qualified to represent me. I search his face, and add, "Somehow, I think you knew."

I must get back to the girls, and we arrange to meet at ten o'clock the following morning.

THE DINING ROOM HAS AN AREA SET ASIDE FOR
passengers to read, play cards, and talk quietly. This
is where I'm to meet Joseph. I'm there early and find
a secluded table for two under a large and somewhat
ornate clock. Tick-tock, tick-tock. The sound is soft,
but in the stillness of my thoughts, it deafeningly
paces my heart. I'm having second thoughts. Is my
wish to adopt the girls genuine? Is it right? Will I
change my mind? No. Is Joseph the right one? Tick-
tock, tick-tock. The minutes drag on as my mind casts
doubt on my every thought.

"I wish to adopt the girls," I hesitate, whisper
when Joseph joins me.

"Lura, do you understand what you're
suggesting?"

"I was certain—I'm certain—but I'm frightened.
Am I doing the right thing? Will I be a good mother?"

"You look exhausted. Have you slept?"

"No. I couldn't sleep. After the girls fell asleep,
I left the cabin and walked until dawn."

"Maybe we should talk later after you've had
some rest."

"No, I need to get this out."

Leaving but one detail out, I explain how Katie
and Ada Mae came into my life. I can see he is
stunned by this revelation. He releases an audible
breath, sits back, and makes a noticeable sound as he
slaps his hands down on his legs. He's taking his
time—stalling—thinking.

"Lura, do you realize what you're saying?"

"Yes, thank you very much," I almost bite his head off. He doesn't deserve my animosity. I add in a softer tone, "I'm ready to do whatever I must."

"Have you asked them?"

"No, not yet."

"Have you considered that they might not want to be adopted?"

"I love them. I can give the girls everything."

"True. But, before you make any decision, you need to know what they want."

Do I really know what they want—what I want? Only moments ago, I was wracked with self-doubt and indecision. I do want to adopt them. Is it the fear that they won't want me that has me so frightened?

"If the girls consent, how long will this take?"

"You may run into a legal issue with the French government over the way you spirited Katie and Ada Mae out of France. What you did could be considered . . . ah . . . kidnapping."

"Kidnapping?"

"If the French authorities had known of the relationship of the girls to the murdered man—their father—they would have taken them into protective custody."

Rules, laws, all made by men who have no idea what women need—deserve. When will it ever change? Even after we get the vote, it will likely remain a country—a world—ruled by men and their egos.

"You men make all the rules, rules for your

convenience, rules you write into laws, laws which you hide behind. Under the French law, which you seem to be championing, the girls would be placed in an orphanage and likely separated. I'm not having any of that."

"I'm not championing any law, for God's sake. If anything, I want to be your champion, and that of the girls."

He stands, takes a few steps away, turns and storms back to the table, his fists clenched. Bending over the table, he points a finger at me for an instant before the wind seems to go out of his sails. He sits and takes several deep breaths. I'm crying. After we take a few minutes to regain our composures, we both apologize and begin again.

"You have to understand that if the French authorities know of the girls' existence and that they are here with you, you can likely expect a confrontation when we arrive in New York."

"They have no authority in America."

"Lura, this is a French-flagged vessel. What if La Sûreté is waiting, boards the ship, and refuses to allow you to take the girls? I'm not sure they can, but they might try."

"You can't allow that to happen. You must not."

"I won't. I promise I won't."

LATER, LONG AFTER DINNER, WE ARE READING IN the cabin. I'm worried about my conversation with

Joseph. What if La Sûreté is waiting and takes the girls? My mind races like one of Father's runaway locomotives. I can't get Joseph's admonition about the French government out of my mind, nor the thought of the girls rebuffing my offer.

Once the girls are finished reading and change into their nightclothes, it's minutes before they are fast asleep. I'm not so lucky. Sitting in the cabin's only chair, I check the clock. It's three in the morning, and for the second night in a row, I'm unable to sleep.

He comes then, as he's wont to do. It's always this way, somewhere in that interlude of time between consciousness—awake—and unconscious-ness—just beyond sleep, almost within my grasp.

"Oh, Walter. What if they don't want me? How could this have happened so fast? I love Katie and Ada Mae as if they were my own. They have become my *raison d'être,* and I cannot, I will not, lose them."

His response isn't what I wanted—hoped. "Lura, darling, as much as I want to help, this is something you must do alone. They will want you or they won't." And then, he's gone.

The remaining hours of night are divided between sporadic sleep, listening to the sounds of the ship, and praying for guidance. "Dear God, please lead me to a life of happiness with these girls. I beg of you. I doubt I can stand another loss so great. Amen."

I wake to the sound of the girls showering and dressing. As much as I want to get the painful question behind me, I don't have the strength to ask them quite yet. Instead, I ask if they are ready for breakfast. Of course, they are.

The dining room is crowded with people and conversation so loud I can't think. I peck at my oatmeal and allow the wonderful Merano coffee to go cold. The girls chatter about the Flying Fish and how they would taste if one happened to fly onto the ship. Ada Mae asks the waiter if the chef would cook the fish for them. He doesn't know and leaves the girls wondering.

Joseph is nowhere to be seen, and I'm somewhat—guiltily—saddened by his absence. Nor do we see him when we take a turn around the promenade.

Returning to our cabin, I tell the girls it's time to read. Ada Mae would prefer to work on her arithmetic. I don't have the energy to help her and insist they read for an hour. Grumbling her assent, she opens her book. Katie's already engrossed in Jim Hawkins' latest challenge in *Treasure Island. Sherlock Holmes* does nothing for me. My mind is in chaos. After fifteen or twenty minutes, I'm still on the same page. The confusion I experience is nothing compared to what's masked.

Ada Mae's trying to stifle a yawn even as she pulls Katie's hair. Katie, in turn, kicks her. What else have I missed, I ask myself as Ada Mae releases her sister's hair and screams, "You brat. I hate you."

"Girls, stop it."

"I hate you, too," Katie yells.

"I said, stop it—now! I have something important to ask you."

The girls go silent in apparent apprehension. Ada Mae drops her work and sits beside me on the bed, more than happy to abandon any pretense of studying. Katie is more hesitant. I don't know if it's because she wants to finish her reading or if she's worried about having a serious conversation. A little of both, perhaps.

"Shouldn't we finish first?" Katie says as she sits next to her sister, taking her hand as she speaks.

"After we talk." My voice barely a whisper.

Resting on the bed, it takes all the strength I can muster to carry on. This is going to be much more difficult than I imagined. My breath comes in gasps, my heart beats like a drum. I'm frightened that they will find my request revolting and want nothing to do with me. I know that isn't true, but I can't help myself; this is all moving so fast. I want it to slow down, put it off, let them come to me. I know in my mind what I must do. It's the fear encumbering my heart that hinders me. Oh, dear God, where is Walter when I need him most? I force down the dread that threatens to overpower me. I'm upsetting the girls. I can't go on like this. I must appear calm, my mind anything but quiet.

"Do you want some water?" Katie asks.

"Please."

I don't want any, I'm not thirsty, but the delay

gives me time to regain my wits. I grasp Mother's pendant so hard the palm of my hand hurts. Katie returns with the water. I take a few tentative sips and then gulp it down, every drop. When I put the glass down, they link their arms in mine. The terror remains—less intense. I want to flee, to hide.

"I would like to make sure of something," I begin, searching their eyes. They are blank, unreadable.

"It's about your father."

They stare, their bodies unmoving. I breathe deeply, twice, three times.

"I told you I would be honored if he were buried at my home. Is that what you want?"

"Miss Lura," says Ada Mae, "thank you, but," she looks at Katie, "we talked to God. He told us to bury Papa with Mama. She's in Boston. That's what Papa would have wanted."

Why didn't I think about their mother and where she lays? Naturally, the girls would want their parents together. Aren't mine together, after all?

"That's a wonderful idea. I'll help you."

The girls both stand and fall, headfirst, into my arms.

"Thank you," they chime.

The way they hold me gives me a feeling of breathless weightlessness, as though I could fly. The fear that has held me in its grasp dissipates as I clasp the girls in a loving embrace. My joy tempered by concern that they may not return my love and what their answer might be to my next question.

"Do you have any other relatives?"

"No," Ada Mae says.

"I know, but it's important that you are sure."

The girls look at each other, their faces scrunched up in concentration. Ada Mae is biting her lip, Katie's eyes close.

"Papa told us his papa was killed in Ireland and that his mama died of the fever. He didn't have any brothers or sisters, nobody else."

"What about your mother."

"Mama was an orphan. She didn't have anybody 'cept us."

No relatives. The fear continues to ebb. It's almost gone when Ada Mae has a question of her own.

"Why do you want to know about Mama and Papa?"

It's a fair question and one that must be answered, but I don't want to blurt out that I want to adopt them. I can't do that, but now is the time to begin the journey.

"Do you know what it means to be adopted?"

"Yes," Katie offers. "Our friend Olivia's mama and papa died of the pox. She didn't have any other family, so they put her in the orphanage with other children who didn't have any family."

"She said that it was scary, and the other girls were mean to her," Ada Mae adds.

"She was there a long time, until Mr. Wilson, the

baker, and his wife brought her home and told Olivia she was their little girl now. They made her work all day and didn't let her go to school like their real little girl."

Their friend's experience has had a disturbing effect on their understanding of adoption. My chest tightens, I struggle for a breath and am not able to stop a furtive tear from sliding down my cheek.

"Not everyone who adopts a child does it to get free work. Most people adopt children because . . . because they love them."

"Do you want to adopt us?" Katie exclaims.

My chest relaxes, breath comes. I have an overwhelming sense of gratitude for this wonderfully sweet child who has asked the question I've been struggling to utter. Tears of joy run wild until I realize she's just asking a question.

"If you want me to."

The girls look at each other—at me—before running into the bathroom and shutting the door. Katie seems to be smiling—positive. Ada Mae is the opposite—dour—negative. What does it mean? Does one want me to adopt her, the other not? Oh, dear Lord, please answer my prayers. Please grant me this one wish. Amen. The fear I had suffered earlier is on the verge of returning. Please, dear God, hear me and grant this wish of mine.

The cabin is small and the door thin. I stare at a small design on it, one I hadn't noticed before. It takes a minute or more for me to realize it's a flower emblem—*fleur-de-lis*. I can hear their voices but can't make out what they are saying. I want to comfort them. Instead, I sit and pray. Praying doesn't seem to be working because it feels like an eternity. I can't keep my eyes off the clock. Tick-tock, tick-tock. It's been ten minutes.

I lie back and stare at the ceiling. I see two things that strike me as odd. The first is a crack that has somehow run from the front to the back of the cabin. That isn't funny; what is, is how it seems to have made itself into a large "W" that touches both sides of the cabin, much like a mountain range.

What are they saying to one another? Please, dear God, give them room in their hearts for me.

The second thing that strikes me as funny is a brown spider. Do they even have spiders on ships? They must have at least one because there's one on the ceiling following the crack as if following a map. I check the clock. Twelve minutes have passed. Tick-tock, tick-tock. Damn it. How long do I have to suffer this interminable wait? At thirteen minutes, the door opens, and the girls walk into the stateroom stopping two feet from me. There is an awkward moment as their faces, red and wet, look down at the floor. After an eternity, Katie looks up.

"Yes," she murmurs.

I want to scream with joy. Instead, I say a silent amen. I'm about to sweep them into my arms, but I see Ada Mae isn't moving. She doesn't look up or speak. Something makes my legs heavy, and my feet lead. Katie nudges Ada Mae, and she finally looks up, locking her eyes on mine. She offers only a barely perceptible nod to me.

It's enough. I'll take it.

TWENTY

WHEN WE ENTER THE DINING ROOM FOR DINNER, the girls can't wait. They run to the table, and it's Ada Mae who tells Joseph I'm going to adopt them and be their new mama.

He rises from his chair and takes both girls into his arms. He twirls them around, their dresses billowing like sheets drying on the line, much to the chagrin of the waiter and the people at the next table, before he lowers them to the floor with a flourish.

I'm so happy, I feel guilty. Joseph looks like he wants to take me in his arms. I want him to. I throw my arms around him and hold him close. My heart flutters in a way I haven't felt since Walter. For a moment, I allow myself to enjoy it before flushing with embarrassment.

"It's alright, Joseph. You'll be their uncle."

"Let's get through the adoption first."

He holds the chair for me as I take my seat.

"I don't know about you ladies, but I do believe this news calls for a celebration."

"Yes, yes," the girls cry as they bounce up and down on their chairs.

"I agree," and imitate the girls bouncing for a second.

The menu is set, as usual, with two choices. This evening the selections are pot roast or baked sea bass; both come with the usual vegetables, steamed brussels sprouts and potatoes. None of the choices seem worthy of a celebratory dinner. The posted dessert is cheesecake. It would be unseemly of me to request special treatment, but special treatment is in order.

"Girls, I left my handbag in the cabin. I would feel ever so much better if I had it here with me. Would you be so kind as to run and get it?"

Without a word, they are up and away. Apparently, it doesn't occur to them that I've left my handbag in our cabin the entire voyage.

Joseph gives me a questioning look.

"We need to arrange something special for the girls. Would you mind asking the dining room manager if he can have a cake prepared along with bowls of ice cream that we can enjoy after we finish our entrees?" Recalling Mr. Benoit's use of bribes, I add, "It may require a small gift, say two-hundred francs."

"Anything for you and the young ladies," he says

with a smile. "Please excuse me for a moment."

Joseph returns with the girls. "Look who we found, Miss Lura. Here's your handbag."

He smiles and nods.

Back in our seats, the waiter takes our orders. I order the fish, Joseph the pot roast, and of course, the girls order the same. Ada Mae doesn't mention the brussels sprouts. When the pot roast arrives, I start to cut Katie's meat for her.

"I can do it myself. Joseph taught me."

This is a day bursting with surprises. Joseph sits up straight, looking as pleased as punch with himself.

"When did this happen?"

"Yesterday."

"Well, Katie, I must say that I'm proud of you. And more than a little surprised that Joseph found time to help you. Thank you, Joseph."

"It was my pleasure."

Once our entrees are cleared away, a cake, complete with candles, arrives, followed by bowls of ice cream. The girls are surprised and show their glee by clapping and laughing.

Joseph explains to the girls that adoption is like the beginning of a new life and should be celebrated with cake and candles. After our party, the four of us take a stroll on deck. It's quite warm, and the sunset is breathtaking. As the orange sphere sinks below the horizon, the sea turns coal black; the effect of the setting sun creates a fiery crown. Layers of evening clouds push the sun's reflection in lines, north and south, almost in a steppingstone pattern, from dark sea to the unmoving blue sky. The sight is spectacular, even more so than the sunrises I enjoyed on the trip east. The girls are not as captivated by the display as Joseph and I are and begin to fidget.

"Once we have you and the girls safely in Ridgeway, the adoption should be a simple matter," Joseph announces as soon as the sun disappears.

How can he be so sweet and so irritating at the same time?

"Can you find your way back to the cabin?" I ask the girls.

"Of course, Miss Lura. Why?" Ada Mae asks.

"I wish to talk to Joseph. When you get to the cabin, I want you to work on your numbers until I return. Understand?" They agree and run hand-in-hand to the door.

Once they are out of sight, I turn to Joseph. My eyes narrow, a loud breath escapes my mouth, and I direct an angry frown toward him.

"What's wrong?"

"Why would you want to discuss the details of the adoption in front of the children?"

He steps back with his hands raised in surprise—surrender—or not. He looks so off-balance, I laugh.

"What's so funny?"

He looks as though he'll explode. I can't stop laughing. It has been an exhilarating evening, but I'm filled with fear, fear that something will block the adoption. I abruptly stop laughing.

"I'm frightened something will go wrong, that I'll lose the girls."

"There could be problems."

"Problems?"

"The French may lodge a formal complaint if they learn you took the children. It's a matter of sovereignty and of face-saving."

"Whose face? These girls are Americans."

"You violated their law."

"What can we do?"

"First, we must get a death certificate or the French equivalent to present in court as proof that the girls are orphans."

A sudden chill sends a shiver through me. I should have told Joseph about Mr. Dean's body.

"Your detective confirmed his death. We'll notify the French Consulate in New York. It'll be a simple matter to request a death certificate from the authorities in Paris."

"There may be a problem."

"What?"

"They no longer have the body."

He looks at me, hands raised, no longer in surrender.

"It's on the way to New York. It might even be on this ship."

He steps away, fists clenched, head back. It's as though he's preparing to fight. Then he steps close—his face ugly—almost bumping into me. In a monotonous voice, deep, slow, menacing, he says,

"You stole the man's body? Jesus."

I consider hitting him. My face screwed up in a fury, I retort, trying to mimic the same controlled manner as he had. "Don't ever speak to me like that," but it comes out a screech, much to my chagrin. Heads turn, ladies stare, men avert their gaze. In my rage, I've forgotten where I am.

"I'm so, so sorry," he says. His face is flushed. Fellow passengers glower at us. "Let's finish this in private, please."

We walk in strained silence to his cabin. I'm surprised how neat the space is. The one clue a man occupies this area is the box of Havana's on the nightstand. I take the single chair, pulling it near the door. Joseph sits on the bed. Even with this arrangement, our knees almost touch.

"I must confess," he says, "that, on the rare occasion, I do have a slight temper."

"I hadn't noticed."

"What you've done regarding Mr. Dean's body—"

"What I did is bring him home for a proper burial."

He rubs his eyes in an insolent manner that makes me want to hit him. What is it with him? He can make me so angry.

"How do you justify the violence you committed upon those men on the train?"

He sits up, surprised by my change of subject. His fingers dig into the flesh of his thighs.

"Those men are thieves who were determined to steal your jewels."

I realize I'm grasping the pendant, holding it against my heart.

"I'm no expert, but I'm sure such a piece could fetch upwards of one hundred thousand francs."

"It was my mother's."

"Then maybe you should wear it concealed when in public. The train was the fourth time I interceded on your behalf."

"Fourth?"

It was Joseph at the Louvre, on the street, and then again on the train. When was there another time? How long has he been watching over— stalking—me?

"The other time was at your hotel."

"My hotel room?"

"The day they followed you on the street, I warned them to stay away. They didn't. That evening while you were at dinner, they entered your room, intending to lie in wait and rob you. I had no choice. I knocked them to the floor and then forced them down the servants' stairwell. I told them that if they accosted you again, I would break their arms."

A surge of heat comes through me like my shoulders are on fire. Am I angry with Joseph, those men, or frightened?

"They didn't believe me."

"On the train, I heard you tell them you had a gun."

He takes out his cigar cutter for me to see.

"This was my gun. One tried to stab me, but I managed to beat them down."

He has been protecting me and the girls for some time now. I guess I should be thankful for his strength and apparent lack of fear. But still—

"I don't understand why you had to break their hands."

"I didn't break their hands for God's sake. Each time they came after you, the level of violence worsened. I feared that if they came again, they might have a gun or other ruffians to help them overcome me and harm you. I had to make sure that didn't happen. I broke a finger on each of their hands so that they couldn't hold a weapon."

"Oh," is all I can manage.

We sit in silence, each lost in thought. I loathe what Joseph did, but I'm surprised to find that I'm not as troubled by his actions as I could be. Not only has he said he wants to be my champion, he has been my champion. Why then, do I get so angry, so easily, with him?

"I understand what you did was for our protection. But that doesn't mean I approve."

"I don't need your approval, nor have I asked for it." Shaking his head at me, he adds, "You are family, and I'll do whatever necessary to protect you . . . and the girls."

We stand and the ship rocks. I stumble somewhat into Joseph's arms, but he steadies me, holding me a moment longer than necessary. The instant his hand moves from my arm, I want it back.

"I apologize . . ." looking down, I say, "for my outburst."

"I'm not angry with you—about what you did—but not you, never you," he says.

TWENTY-ONE

OUR FINAL NIGHT AT SEA, I PROMISE THE GIRLS we'll be up and on deck when we sight land. This means getting up and dressed long before sunrise.

As a special treat, Joseph somehow arranges for us to have access to the first-class deck. The girls, exhausted but excited, begin the day with cups of delicious hot chocolate. Joseph and I enjoy the exquisite Merano coffee. Standing at the forward end of the ship, we don't get the sunrise experience that I enjoyed on the trip to Europe. Joseph has a spot at the railing that allows us to look back to the east, but the girls are unimpressed by the sight of the sun rising and turn their gaze west for a glimpse of the distant New York coast as it rises above the horizon in the glow of the morning sun. It isn't long until the offshore breeze carries the scent—odor—of New York to us. After the fragrance of the clean salt air of the open sea, the stench is odious.

Several hours later, we transit The Straits. The fog is heavy, and I'm relieved to see we already have tugboats alongside to guide us to the dock. The harbor is not much cleaner or better smelling than Le Havre. The smoke from the factories, processing plants, coal-burning vessels, and the thousands of garbage-burning barrels joins together to foul the air and leave a coat of filth on everything. Even our ship has a lewd layer as thin as mist left on a mirror by one's breath. By the time we dock, the fog clears, replaced by a cold and gusty wind.

Now is the time of our greatest danger. Our luggage taken away, all that remains is for us to disembark. Joseph will remain nearby in the event we need him. I haven't told the girls of my concern, but they seem to be aware that something more than arriving in New York is going on.

The chill deepens my fear of losing the girls to La Sûreté. It intensifies as the line of passengers nears the disembarkation official. My knees almost buckle. I clutch Joseph's arm, and he stops, keeping me upright.

He puts his hand over mine. "Be brave," he whispers before stepping back a few paces, placing several other passengers between us.

The girls are the picture of sweetness—wide-eyed—scared by circumstance into best behavior as am I.

A uniformed and officious French functionary

scrutinizes my travel documents. He takes his time. It's as if he's reading each word. After what seems a lifetime, he calls over another man—in a suit—and hands him my papers. This man turns them over and spends several minutes examining the front and back of each document. I have an envelope with one-thousand francs in my handbag, but something tells me that this is one time that Mr. Benoit would advise against offering a bribe.

He stops and looks up at me several times, turns his head with a narrowing of his eyes, and gazes at the girls. I didn't experience this kind of scrutiny when traveling first class where I was waved through with barely a glance. After what seems an eternity, he raises his eyes to mine. "Madame Myer, I see that you traveled alone to France."

"Yes," I say, my voice cracking.

"Who are these girls who now travel with you?"

"My nieces."

"Aunt Lura," Katie pipes up, tugging at my coat, "please hurry. I see Papa waving from the dock. Please."

"Papa," Ada Mae screams.

The official looks at her and Katie waving toward the pier. There must be a hundred men waving at passengers. With an audible "Hmm," he hands my papers back to the uniformed official, who, in turn, hands them to me, grunts, and waves us away. The girls and I hurry down the gangplank.

Moments later, Joseph ambles down, a sly grin on his face.

GIOVANNI BARTOLINI AND LOUIS BRANDEIS ARE waiting at the foot of the gangway. Giovanni is wearing a dark topcoat buttoned to the neck and a top hat pulled down low. I recognize the weave of his coat immediately as Donegal tweed from the various pieces of colored yarn woven here and there into the cloth. It's fashionable and attractive. Wringing gloved hands, Giovanni's eyes dart from me to the ship and back. I've never seen him so nervous.

Brandeis is at least four inches taller than Giovanni, and years younger, closer to my age, I presume. He's wearing a hideous green windowpane English tweed, a style currently returning to fashion with the dandies. From the way he's standing, one arm holding the other, constantly twisting his neck and drumming his foot up-and-down, I assume he's agitated, probably about his unwanted involvement in the way he was trapped into helping, illegally, bring a body into the country. I step up to Giovanni, expecting a warm hug, but he bows and steps aside.

"Mrs. Myer, I believe you remember Mr. Brandeis."

Mr. Brandeis, scowling, welcomes me with barely concealed annoyance. I'm aware that I've caused him a great deal of aggravation, particularly in the matter of Mr. Dean's body, in the brief time he has represented me, but ignoring the rules of common courtesy? I will not be treated in this manner. I direct a curt nod in his direction before turning my back to him.

"Joseph, girls, I want you to meet my dear friend, Mr. Giovanni Bartolini."

Joseph walks with Ada Mae and Katie holding their hands. As he steps up to Giovanni, he releases the girls, and the two men shake hands.

Joseph, all smiles, turns to Mr. Brandeis, and the two men embrace. Mr. Brandeis glowers at me over Joseph's shoulder.

"Louis, I haven't seen you since that bout between John L. Sullivan and Charlie Mitchell last year. I should never have bet on the Irishman."

"Taking your money was my pleasure, Joseph."

"And what of my money?" I chime in, rudely.

Joseph corrects his posture, opening his arms in an attempt to lower the hostility so evident between Mr. Brandeis and me.

"We'll have to pay another visit to Madison Square Garden, and soon. But, now, we ought to get down to business."

"Joseph, when I agreed to represent Mrs. Myer," Brandeis says, ignoring me completely, "I had no idea you two were related. Had I known, I would have suggested that you handle her affairs." Looking about and still ignoring me, he says, "We should press on to my firm where we can address Mrs. Myer's situation in the privacy of my office."

Giovanni and I exchange looks of frustration. Do these two think they are at a private club enjoying conversation over cigars and brandy? I'm livid with anger.

"Gentlemen, the girls and I are standing here, are we not? Must I remind you that you're here to represent me and my interests and that you are well compensated for it."

Brandeis frowns, but Giovanni and Joseph look down at their shoes.

"We can continue this conversation, with me as part of it, in my hotel suite once the girls have been cared for."

Nobody moves.

"Have I made myself clear?"

"Lura," stammers Giovanni, "I've reserved a suite at the Waldorf. And you needn't worry. You've not stayed in this suite."

"Thank you."

"You're welcome. I've seen to your baggage and that of Mr. Myer. I took the liberty of booking him into the Waldorf as well. I have a carriage waiting for us and a cab standing by for the gentlemen."

Ignoring the two lawyers, I take Giovanni's elbow. "Shall we go?"

"I'll not need lodging, Mr. Bartolini," Joseph says. "I have an apartment here."

I do not want to be separated from Joseph, however irritating he may be. He must come with us, even if I must play on his sympathies and sense of chivalry.

The girls leave him and run to me, shouting, "Miss Lura, please, we want to be with Joseph. Make him come with us."

God love the girls; this display makes my request

that much harder for him to refuse.

"Joseph, I would feel safer if you would stay near the girls and me for a few days. At least until we know what obstacles we face."

"Madam, your wish is my command."

The girls laugh. He bows, and as he straightens, gives them an exaggerated wink. It's more than they can stand. They run to him and throw their arms around him.

"Allow me to escort you to your carriage, me ladies."

The three follow Giovanni, leaving Mr. Brandeis and me alone.

"Well, Mrs. Myer, you seem to have had quite an adventure."

"Have you decided not to abandon me to my just desserts?"

"No, madam. I'll not abandon you. I must tell you, though, I'm mightily displeased with some of your actions."

"That's fair. I *may* have been somewhat reckless."

He shakes his head, though his facade begins to fade. The tightest little smile curls his lips.

"Madam, you stretch the meaning of the word."

TWENTY-TWO

GIOVANNI AND EMILY, THE ONLY CATHOLICS among us, traveled ahead to Boston to help with the funeral arrangements for the girls' father.

Arriving at the church the day before the funeral, I'm pleased with the appearance of the small edifice. Ninety-year-old Saint Stephen's Church is built of red brick with a facade of white columns. The structure is topped with a great clock tower holding the belfry. A sweltering summer day outside, the temperature inside is surprisingly agreeable. Not just for us, but also the mice scurrying away from the open door.

There are pews to seat no more than one hundred. The altar is covered with a magnificent embroidered tapestry. I'm surprised to see six small windows, three on each side of the nave. They are beautifully constructed of stained glass with scenes of Christ and the Virgin Mary.

Giovanni introduces me to Monsignor O'Sullivan, who will conduct the funeral mass. The man is short, rotund, with rosy cheeks, a bulbous red nose, and a strange-looking beard under his chin that covers his throat. From his appearance and the stink of whiskey on his breath, I deduce he is fond of his drink.

"Please, Mrs. Myer," he takes my arm, "allow me to show you our lovely church and tell you a little of its history."

I'm not the least interested in the history of this or any other Catholic church. But before I can convey that to the priest, Giovanni signals me to feign interest.

"But of course, Monsignor. I would be honored."

He drags me around the church, going on and on about the most mundane of details.

"The cornerstone was laid September 23, 1802, by the Congregationalists as the New North Church. Unlike our Catholic churches and cathedrals, it was built in a perfect square, seventy-two by seventy-two. The property was acquired by the Archdiocese of Boston in 1862 and consecrated as Saint Stephen."

"Quite interesting," I say, although my mind has wandered back to the April day Walter and I were married in another and far more modest church. I even recall how the fat summer flies buzzed against the colored glass, and how the ladies' fans caught the sunshine making everything flicker. Father told me that the noise of all those fans made it difficult for him to hear Pastor Carter. The memory brings a smile to my face.

"Ah, listen to me going on and on. This isn't why you're here. Why don't you and Mr. Bartolini come with me to the parish office?"

He leads the way, and we go through a dark, musky corridor and down to a basement room with an ochre door. The office is so small, there is scarcely enough room for the priest and me to sit. Giovanni is forced to stand in the doorway.

"I understand the arrangements for internment have been finalized with North Cambridge Catholic Cemetery."

"Yes, Monsignor. Mr. Dean is to be buried next to his wife."

"Will his body be at the wake?"

"Wake?" asks Giovanni. "We . . . ah, ah . . . there are . . . we have no plans for a wake," he says to the priest.

"But I understand there's one planned for this evening," the priest says, turning to me. "Members of his old . . . shall I say business associates . . . have announced a wake to be held in his honor at O'Toole's Tavern. It's but a short walk from here."

"A tavern?"

"Mr. Dean didn't have a home where a vigil would normally be held. Mr. O'Toole has offered the use of his establishment."

"We shall not be in attendance."

Had I known of the desire for such an event, I would have prohibited it. My God, have these heathens no boundaries?

The priest's annoyance shows in the tone he uses. "Of course, your attendance isn't required, but tradition—you must realize—tradition calls for the family to be present. Mr. Dean's friends will take offense if his daughters are not there."

"I don't give a whit what those hooligans wish. They are likely the ones who had Mr. Dean murdered. They can have their wake, but the girls will not attend, nor will Mr. Dean's body be there for them to gloat over."

Giovanni—always the good Catholic and fearful of the power of the clergy—coughs. He must want me to acquiesce or at least seem to, but I owe nothing to this priest.

"The sole purpose of this funeral is to allow the girls to say goodbye to their father," I say as if giving a command. I follow in a softer tone with, "During the procession from the church to the cemetery, the girls and I will ride in a carriage behind the hearse with armed detectives to protect us should there be an attempt to interfere in any way."

"I understand, Mrs. Myer," the Monsignor says in a slow voice as if talking to a child. "Whether you attend the wake or not, is your prerogative."

I should tell the fool-headed and pompous old man what I think, but it would do nothing to improve the situation. Priests—among the most unenlightened men in positions of power—have spoken to women in this outrageous manner—this damnable manner—for centuries. The day will come when women will take their rightful place in the world.

"Nevertheless, many of his friends and acquaintances will be here for the funeral mass. The girls should be prepared to receive words of condolence."

"The girls will speak with none of the criminals. Not as long as they are in my care." Even as I say this, I realize that this is beyond my purview. It will be up to Ada Mae and Katie, not me.

"There is another matter of importance—most delicate." The priest puts his hands together.

"What might that be?" the tenor of my voice insolent.

"Yes, Monsignor?" Giovanni steps in, noticing my growing impatience.

"There are some who would say that Mr. Dean was a manifest sinner, and a Mass for the Dead might bring scandal upon the church."

"So," I say as I walk out, done with this fool. "The same could be said of your Mr. O'Toole."

"A suitable donation—"

"I shall take my leave now," I say without holding back the anger evident in my voice. "If you require an even larger donation, you may call for Mr. Bartolini at the Parker House."

THE DAY OF THE BURIAL IS BEAUTIFUL, DAWNING clear, and comfortable. Although we didn't publicize the funeral, word has spread throughout the community. Johanna Guntner, a female Pinkerton Detective, tells me members of the Irish underworld will attend. I'm loathe to expose the girls to these villains but accept the fact that some things are beyond my control. A beauty, Mrs. Guntner is six feet tall and judging by her diction, well educated. Female detectives are extremely rare. Born ten years after Allan Pinkerton hired his first female detective in 1856, she looks older than her twenty-eight years. I assume it's the result of the hard life a detective must live. From occasional comments, she makes— universally misinterpreted by men—she's a strong feminist and suffragette. I like her.

The funeral mass is scheduled for two in the afternoon. I want to keep the girls distracted, and I am glad we have time to see some of the city. I ask them where they would like to go.

"Swan boats at Boston Common," squeals an excited Katie.

"I don't see why not. Besides, I've always wanted to see a swan boat. Do they fly?"

As soon as I say this, I see that Ada Mae's lower lip is trembling. I bend down and ask, "What's the matter?"

"Papa loved flowers. He always wanted a garden of his own. We went on picnics by the statute of George Washington."

"No," Katie yelps. "I want to go to the swan boats."

"That isn't the way a lady acts."

"I'm not a lady."

"Another outburst like that and you will stay at the hotel."

She may not be happy, but at least she quiets down.

"If we get Joseph to come with us, we can go now and be back in time for lunch."

"Yes, ma'am."

"Then it's settled. Let's go find your uncle."

The Garden Park and the swan boats prove to be a pleasant diversion. For a few hours, we relax and delight in the beauty of Boston. We even manage to find some French Chew. We lose track of time until Katie announces that she's hungry.

After finishing frankfurters, supposedly a German treat, which I consider an abomination, Joseph suggests we get back to the hotel.

We arrive with scarcely enough time to change into mourning clothes. I quit wearing the depressing garments not long after Emily and Earl rescued me from my deep despair. Still officially in my year of mourning, I wear the black crape dress with matching bonnet and parasol I wore to Father's funeral. Ada Mae wears a dark purple knee-length dress with matching stockings. Katie wears the same style dress but in gray. Because of their ages, I won't subject them to the indignity of uncomfortable and ugly hats.

THE CARRIAGE RIDE TO THE CHURCH IS CRAMMED with the four of us plus Mrs. Guntner and one of the male detectives. I'm worried about how the Irish ruffians will behave.

"The wake wasn't the drunken brawl we feared it was going to be," Mrs. Guntner tells me. She assures me that she has a suitable number of Pinkertons available to quash any fracas at the church or the cemetery, should the need arise.

"I'll be with you and the girls until you are safely back at the hotel." Her words are a comfort.

Ada Mae retreats as much as possible in the cramped carriage. When I give her a questioning look and ask if she's ill, she snaps her head to the side and refuses to speak. She remains unresponsive all the way to the church.

Katie whimpers, her head in my lap. My heart is heavy, and I share their sorrow. Overwhelming wretchedness once again threatens to crush me. Joseph must see what's happening, for he gives my shoulder the gentlest of squeezes, and I know I'll survive. I'll be strong for Ada Mae and Katie. The coach pulls to a halt; we're at the church.

"Please give us a minute. I wish to speak with the girls."

Joseph and the detective exit the carriage and leave us alone.

"Now," I say, placing a hand on each of the girls' knees, "let's wipe away the tears and show everyone how brave we are." Katie bursts into tears and mumbles something unintelligible. Ada Mae wipes the tears from Katie's face with her hanky.

"I want Papa," Katie cries, pressing her face against my bosom.

THE SERVICE IS LONG AND BORING. AS A CHRISTIAN and lifelong Methodist Episcopal, I'm used to ceremony and lengthy services, but, never, not on his best of days, did Pastor Carter ever come close to competing with the long-winded Monsignor for pomp and circumstance. The procession bringing Mr. Dean's casket into the church is slow, painfully slow. Monsignor O'Sullivan's long-practiced ritual with the delivery of the burning incense is unhurried—exaggerated—meticulous. The service begins with the blessing of Mr. Dean and his soul, followed by a series of readings and incantations in Latin. Father had insisted I read the archaic language. I know enough to follow most of what he says.

"Eternal rest give to them, O Lord, and let perpetual light shine upon them," the priest repeats the Introit in English.

After the reading of the Psalms and the Gospel, he delivers a short sermon in English. Before communion, there's a eulogy by Mr. Patrick O'Toole. I hadn't expected this, and certainly not from Paddy O'Toole. He's particularly loquacious, speaking for nigh on to an hour. Even Monsignor O'Sullivan shows visible signs of irritation.

"What right does this murdering thug have to speak at the funeral of the man he had killed?"

"It was too crowded and noisy for him to speak at the wake," whispers Giovanni. "I believe he made a special contribution to the church—the Monsignor—for the privilege."

"So, a murderer can buy both a pulpit to talk about his victim and forgiveness for his sins. It's little wonder most of the world hates Catholics."

"Lura, you can't condemn the entire religion because of the acts of a few."

THE MORNING AFTER THE FUNERAL, GIOVANNI and Emily take the girls to Faneuil Hall, giving Joseph and me a chance to talk. We take a stroll along the avenue. Unable to get the funeral, and Patrick O'Toole, out of my mind, I'm filled with apprehension. Will this evil man come after the girls or me for interfering with his plans? Joseph must sense my anxiety, for he takes my arm and guides me to a small sidewalk café where he orders coffee. I can't put my fears into words. Joseph holds my hand, and we sit quietly, breathing the sweet fragrance before sipping the strong liquid. Our table faces a small garden. The serenity and his silence allow my anxiety to lessen. Nodding my head to signal my well-being, I stand, and we walk, arm-in-arm, back to the Parker House.

For convenience and privacy, I have room service deliver coffee and tea to my suite. After pouring, Joseph mentions he thinks the funeral went well.

"Whatever do you mean?" I'm being horrible, but I can't let go of the fear I have of Paddy O'Toole and his Irish thugs.

Joseph stiffens and turns to the window. His exhalation is long and audible. He seems to be lost in thought before he clasps his hands over his chest and says, "There was not one problem. Every person there, and remember it was crowded to the point of standing room only, was quiet and respectful."

I force myself to pick up the teapot and fill his cup. The ritual of it, the practiced repetition, demands mindfulness and concentration and frees me from my anger. By the time I finish pouring the tea, I'm sporting a smile as a peace offering.

"I'll stick with coffee," he says, "and we should move on to the matter of the adoption."

"Joseph, I won't be staying in New York. I've been away from Grisham Manor far too long, and it's time for the girls to settle into a vestige of normalcy."

"What of the adoption?" He almost spills his coffee as his head snaps up and his cup tips.

"I'm well known in Ridgefield and Hartford, and no doubt the judges in Connecticut will be kindly disposed to the Myer name, if not my money. I have no ties to New York."

"Please tell me this is the last surprise you have for me, at least until the girls are no longer a problem."

"The girls are not a problem," I whisper, "the adoption is."

"Maybe it would be better if I were to remain in New York. I know of several competent lawyers in Connecticut." He takes a sip of his coffee. "I would be delighted to recommend one."

"That might be necessary." I stress might in the same tone he used with delighted.

He sets his coffee down, shrinks into his chair. His hands open and drop to his lap.

Have I gone too far? I want equality, not dominance.

"If you approve, I'll come to Connecticut."

"Will you continue to represent us?"

"If you wish."

"I do." All anger gone from my voice—my heart. A sense of loss overcomes me at the thought of Joseph remaining in New York. I want this man, my brother-in-law, close. And, of course, near the girls. Why do I feel so conflicted?

"For now," his voice more assured, "you do have a level of influence in Connecticut that would be lacking in New York. I'll take the lead on the adoption as Louis and Giovanni are engaged in the consolidation and liquidation of your holdings."

"How are they doing?"

"You couldn't have found two men more fitted to work together. Giovanni has an uncanny understanding of people and problems. He's a natural arbiter. Coupled with Louis's legal genius, I believe you have an invincible combination."

"I'm sure you will be as capable with the adoption."

His eyes narrow, and when he sees I'm smiling. "You're such an . . . oh . . . I don't know what." He can no longer maintain his anger. "When do we leave for Grisham Manor?"

"Tomorrow. By train. Please ask Giovanni to keep the detectives near until we're safely home."

"Does it give you pleasure to vex me?" he says, shaking his head and failing to conceal a bourgeoning smile.

THE TRIP HOME IS EXHILARATING. FOR ONCE, THE wind keeps the smoke from filling the passenger cars, and we have a wonderful view of the countryside. The farms, even though small, are larger than those in France. The stone fences are higher, better maintained, and newer by hundreds of years. The girls tell me the only times they have been on a train before were the trips to and from Le Havre to Paris, both at night. Leaning out the windows, they shout about every new sight. Their excitement is infectious, and I learn they have never been outside a city. From Boston to Hartford, we travel on the New England Railroad.

I tell the girls, "My father built and owned one of the smaller railroads that became part of the Boston, Hartford and Erie. He sold his share for a handsome profit. After BH&E bankrupted in 1893, it was reorganized and became the New York and New England."

"Will we ride it to Grisham Manor?"

"No, Katie. We change trains in Stamford, and then we'll take a carriage from Ridgefield to the manor."

Shortly after we change trains, the wind abates as we snake into a dense forest, and smoke pours in through the windows covering everything with soot. Ada Mae's racked by coughs. I cover her face with a damp handkerchief while Emily does the same for Katie. Giovani and Joseph close the compartment windows in a futile attempt to keep the smoke out. I watch their eyes water and their faces grimace in misery, my discomfort mitigated by the thought that my father built this stretch of rail to Ridgefield, and Joseph doesn't realize that unless I sell, someday it will belong to the girls.

In Ridgefield, we bid goodbye to Giovanni, Emily, and the Pinkertons. I'm exhausted after the day-long trip and can't wait to get home and soak in a hot bath. Arriving at Grisham Manor, Ada Mae and Katie want to explore the property and pet the horses and lambs they see in the pasture.

"Not tonight." Beyond exhaustion, I mean what I say. "You will have plenty of time to explore tomorrow. Now, we are going to eat, bathe, and get some rest."

"Amen," says Joseph.

"I'm hungry," Ada Mae shouts. The girls always

seem to be hungry.

As if by magic, Earl appears.

"Miss Lura, Cook has prepared a light repast for you and your guests in the great room," he says with the warmth I've known my entire life. I love him as I would a favorite uncle.

"Thank you, Earl. Please tell Cook we shall be there momentarily."

"Thank you, Miss Lura," he whispers and leaves as silently as he came.

"Earl has been here my entire life. Cook—she insists on being called Cook—has been with us almost as long." I doubt if anyone other than Earl knows her given name. "She is a wonderful cook. Let's not keep her waiting."

Cook looks the way she has for the last twenty years. She's wearing a dress of light gray cotton with an apron and small cook's bonnet. The apron is unlike any usually associated with a cook. It isn't a single color, neither the white nor beige ordinarily worn by kitchen staff, but multicolored and as bright as the smile on her face.

"Miss Lura, it's so wonderful to have you home."

She hustles across the room, grabs me in a very un-servant-like hug, and plants kisses on both my cheeks, which I return with equal exuberance. I can tell Earl would like to do the same, but his position demands restraint. I'm not so restrained, so I hug and kiss him.

Finishing the meal of hot soup and drained of my last bit of energy, all I want is to escape to my room and sleep. I look to Earl for help with the girls. As always, he knows what needs to be done and has already issued orders for the maid to draw me a hot bath and sees that Joseph's settled in one of the guest rooms.

Undressing in the room I once shared with Walter, I stare at our bed. The bed where our child—Little George—was conceived. Overcome by emotion, and at last alone, I cry. Soaking in the tub, I am aware of the pain draining away. I remain there until the water cools, and I begin to shiver. Pulling on an old and comfortable dressing gown, I slip between familiar sheets and am asleep within minutes.

When I wake, it's morning. The bath, a good cry, and a good night's sleep give me a feeling of exultation.

I'm ready for anything.

TWENTY-THREE

THE STEAMING HOT COFFEE AND WARM BREAD
pudding with bananas Cook has for me in the
breakfast nook make for an ideal way to start the day.
Joseph's there, sitting where Father and I had spent
so many pleasant mornings talking of politics and his
plans for the railroad, each day in a different language.
He's engrossed in reading something. His being there
gives me an ever so warm and comfortable feeling. I
visit with Cook about the evening meal, leaving him
in peace. He must hear us, for he stands. I tell him to
sit and join him. He seems distracted.

"Joseph, I hope you slept as well as I did. Are
you alright? You haven't touched your breakfast, and
your coffee must be cold."

He looks at me but doesn't say anything.

"Cook made it special. She gets the bananas
from Emily, who gets them from New York."

"I have a message from Brandeis." He takes a sip of his coffee. "You're right. It's gone cold. The news is disturbing."

"What?" The joy, so powerful moments before, begins to drain from my heart.

"The French have lodged a formal protest with the American Ambassador in Paris."

"How can that be?"

"They claim you stole the body of Francis Dean and unlawfully removed it from France."

My mouth opens, but he is already shaking his head.

"I'm not sure we can deny taking the body. After all, we buried him."

Holding back tears, all I can think of is taking the girls and running away. I got them out of France. There are countries where I can buy a new name and start a fresh life with the girls. Would Joseph come with us? Would we marry? I have more than enough money to go anywhere in the world. But where would we go? I love my home. Would I, could I, learn to love a home in a strange new country with unfamiliar cultures and new languages? Even English-speaking countries speak different English than we do here in America, here at home. What of the girls? Would they grow to hate me for separating them from America? I doubt it, but I would miss Grisham Manor and all the people, alive and dead, I so deeply love. Would I learn to hate the girls for my decision to choose them over my home? Oh, God, what am I to do? What of

Joseph, and what would he think? I do not run from problems like I did when Walter and Little George died. I will not—cannot—run again, ever.

"They also claim you kidnapped Katie and Ada Mae and demand you release them to the French Embassy in New York or face prosecution. You could face serious charges. Whatever the resolution, it's likely you will never be allowed to return to France on pain of arrest."

I'm about to say something in my defense when Earl announces that a French officer has arrived and wishes to speak with me.

"Where is he?"

"I've taken the liberty of escorting him to the great room."

"Please ask him to wait a moment."

"This must have to do with the girls," I needlessly say to Joseph.

"It's unlikely he knows what we've done with their father's body."

"We?"

"We're in this together now." He shakes his head. "I'm your attorney. Be careful what you say."

The officer, attired in the formal dress of the French Army, hands me a large official-looking packet with several seals and the notation, *Communiqué Officiel Republique Francaise*. Breaking the wax seals, I open it and read the document, written in English, it contains and then hand it to Joseph.

"Madame Myer, might I inquire as to when

you intend to deliver the young ladies to my government?"

If I answer him, I'll likely blaspheme.

"Captain," Joseph intercedes, "Mrs. Myer simply escorted two young Americans back to their home country."

"Monsieur, this is a matter of honor to my country. I'm but a simple soldier delivering a message and asking for a response that my superiors will understand and accept. I hope Madame will allow both our countries to resolve the matter in a manner amicable to all."

I want to speak, but Joseph squeezes my hand.

"I'm Mrs. Myer's attorney," he says. I feel my temper rising. But his tone is so assured and officious. "All communications with your government shall be between their representative and me."

The French officer looks at me, his face expressionless. I want to scream. Speaking up would not only embarrass Joseph but me as well. I raise my chin. Releasing my arm, Joseph asks me to give him and the captain a few minutes. The last thing I want to do is leave the fate of the girls in the hands of these two men. However, I realize Joseph is my lawyer, and I must trust him.

"If you find a need for me, ring for Earl. He'll locate me."

JOSEPH MYER

The great room of Grisham Manor is one of the most beautiful I've seen outside a first-class hotel or castle. The ceilings are at least ten feet tall. The walls are painted white, but for the most part, covered with exquisitely carved woodwork. There are several varieties, but mahogany dominates. Such a room could be dark and foreboding, but not this one. It's warm, comfortable—gives the sense of being lived in—the center of the home. The fireplace, taller and wider than my height, is as large as the bedroom in the small New York apartment that serves as my home and office. I wonder how Walter felt in this room, this house. Birth gave him a higher station in life than me, but nothing compared to this. How did he deal with the sudden wealth that came with his marriage to Lura? How would I? I tell myself to stop fantasizing—I'm her lawyer, not her suitor—represent her. Fortunately, I was here when the French officer arrived. It gives us . . . us . . . I'm, referring to Lura and me as us. Stop it.

"Captain, if I may introduce myself, I'm Joseph Myer, and I represent Mrs. Myer as well as Katie and Ada Mae Dean. Mrs. Myer intends to adopt the girls and raise them as her own." Damn, I sound like a pompous ass.

The officer smiles, makes a pretense of a bow, and in an officious tone of self-importance, says, "Bien Monsieur. I'm Captain Julien Victor Eugène Delacroix. Like you, I'm an attorney. That is one of the reasons I was selected to deliver my government's communiqué to Madame Myer."

"I appreciate your government's concern. It must be an honor for a man of your position to be entrusted with such an assignment."

If he doesn't begin to show some respect, I might lose my temper and challenge the peacock to a round or two. The thought of him lying bloodied at my feet brings a smile to my face.

"Bien. My superiors have detailed me to act as a conduit. Until we resolve this unfortunate situation, I shall take rooms in town."

He seems to have not heard my insult or has otherwise chosen to ignore the offense.

"What, might I ask, is your intent?" I ask. "Will I be forced to employ armed men to protect Mrs. Myer and the girls from action by you or your government?"

Delacroix takes a step back and grips his Kepi, twisting the stiff uniform hat. I can't tell if he's angry, embarrassed, or both. Have I gone too far?

"*Bien sur pas, Monsieur.*" After a momentary pause, Delacroix continues. "We are civilized people. We will let our courts and our ambassador resolve this with their counterparts here in America. I'm offended you would suggest such a vile course of action between our countries." His voice rises in anger. "We are allies, after all."

"I didn't intend to offend you or your country, Captain. I merely wish to understand your position and that of your government." Why am I so rude? This soldier is merely carrying out his orders.

He licks his lips and looks somewhere over my shoulder. It's obvious he's a proud man and that my words didn't succeed as an apology. Of course not. It wasn't an apology. I'm allowing my frustration to show through in my insolent behavior. Openness— full honesty—that's the only thing that will work with this man.

"I apologize for my ill-mannered affront."

He makes eye contact; his demeanor loosens, nimbleness returns to his motions.

"I understand your concerns," Delacroix responds in a more approachable tone. "You have my word as an officer and gentleman. No such action will occur. My orders are to be available as needed, even to offer protection to Mrs. Myer and the girls should they face any danger or inconvenience."

There's a great deal more to Captain Delacroix than I first imagined.

"Captain, if you please, I would like to confer with my client before you and I talk further. Can we meet over lunch tomorrow?"

"That would be my pleasure."

"Fine. It's settled. I'll call on you at noon."

"Monsieur, if it pleases you, there's one other matter, somewhat delicate."

What could be more delicate than his government's demand for the return of the girls?

"Yes, Captain?"

"There is the matter of girls' father. Can you tell me what has become of his body? It was unlawfully spirited away from the morgue in Paris."

"I can tell you that Mr. Dean's remains are buried alongside those of his wife."

"Am I to assume somewhere outside of France?"

"Yes, Boston. More than that, I can't say."

"Bien. I shall advise my superiors."

I call for Earl, and we walk Delacroix out to the porte-cochère. I watch the captain's carriage turn onto the main road and remain standing long after his dust settles.

Why am I here when I should be in New York serving my established clients? What is it about Lura that captivates my every thought? Despite her maddening nature—the problems she has dragged me into—I feel a growing attachment to her.

THE NIGHT IS COMFORTABLY WARM, AND I OPEN the windows and draw back the curtains. Cloudless, it should be cold, but it's not. The moon is full and bright, silhouetting the barn and allowing me to see for miles. This is a wonderful home, and Lura will make a wonderful mother. I must make her dreams come true, not just for her sake, but for that of the girls as well. Crawling into bed, I fall asleep determined to succeed in bringing those events to fruition.

I wake to the melodic sound of morning birds, something I never hear in New York. Going to the window, the warble of barn swallows is the most distinct. I know they're there; last evening I saw several of their mud nests under the eaves of the barn. Several orange-breasted robins are strutting their stuff with their unique cheer-up song. I would love to live in a place like this. There's a gentle tap at the door. I pull on my robe and open the door. The maid's there with a tray which she places on the desk.

"Coffee and hot rolls," she says in reply to my questioning look. "Cook sent them."

This courtesy is unexpected, but welcome. After thanking the maid, I pour a cup of the steaming liquid. I can't dally over the treat. I must dress and prepare for my meeting with the French officer.

I join Lura in the kitchen and enjoy another cup of coffee before calling for Earl. I ask him if there's a saddle horse I can use. His response surprises me.

"Mr. Myer, it would be inappropriate for a man of your stature to meet with an emissary of a foreign government dressed in riding apparel. If you will be so kind as to change into suitable attire, I have arranged transportation."

When I change, Earl's waiting at the porte-cochère with a Hamshaw Cabriolet. Designed for two passengers and pulled by one horse, it's one of the finest carriages ever built. This one is in immaculate condition. I guess it to be about four years old and say so to Earl.

"You know what it is?"

"I do," smiling good-naturedly at his skepticism. "I'm surprised you have one." Flaunting my knowledge, I add, "It was manufactured by Hamshaw Coach Works of Leicester, England. How did it get here?"

"Mister George brought it back from England." I can see pride in Earl's face. "He also kept a Tilbury. The Tilbury was his first carriage. He had it long before he married Mrs. Grisham. Even though it can be dangerous, it's a wonder over rough roads, and it's Miss Lura's favorite."

We spend a few minutes examining the carriage and discussing its craftsmanship. Realizing that if I don't hurry, I'll be late for my meeting, I thank Earl for his kindness and climb into the carriage. He mentions he left the folding hood down because the day is so pleasant. I assure him if the weather turns bad, I know how to raise it. He gives me directions to the village and the hotel. The drive takes but minutes.

THE HOTEL HAS A LIMITED LUNCH MENU. CAPTAIN Delacroix and I both order the peppered lamb with a minty butter bean mash.

We've been served iced teas and our salads when over Delacroix's left shoulder, I spy a small heart. Deep and crudely gouged into the faded paint of the old wall, it captures my fancy. There are no initials to provide a hint of who might have etched this symbol of love. Who did this unknown man love? Could a woman have scratched it? When?

"Monsieur Myer," Delacroix says, breaking the spell and bringing me back from my daydream. "Our balcony perch allows us a small amount of privacy and a magnificent view of the main street." After a pause, he adds, "Is your carriage from the realm of Her Royal Majesty, the good Queen Victoria?"

"It is. Why do you ask?"

"Even though Hamshaw carriages are made in England, they are very popular in my country. My father and I each own one."

"How so?"

"A few years ago, I had an assignment in England and took the opportunity to visit the Hamshaw Coach Works. With a loan from Father, I purchased four."

"Four?"

"Upon returning to France, I sold two, and the profit paid for our two. If Peugeot's horseless carriages weren't coming into vogue, we would have bought and sold several additional carriages."

We find even more shared experiences as we discuss the carriage and previous trips to London and the Orient. From different countries and classes, the two of us have much more in common than the mere fact that we are lawyers. Despite our difference and the potential litigation that separates us, I would like to count Delacroix amongst my friends.

Finished with our meal, we order brandy and

cigars and turn to the business at hand. He assures me France's demand for the return of Katie and Ada Mae isn't a frivolous claim, far from it. "My government has strong feelings about the sovereignty of our nation and the sanctity of our laws."

"I understand."

"My instructions are to oppose any attempt you contemplate that doesn't coincide with our demands."

Delacroix doesn't mean this as a threat. However, it does give me cause for concern. What the hell does he have in mind? Maybe I should call the Pinkertons back, at least until I know more about his intentions.

"Your brandy isn't very good."

"What?" This sudden change of subject catches me off guard.

"It lacks the excellence of our fine French brandies, even as we recover from the Great Blight, which was caused by a gift from your country, I might add."

I could take offense; after all, he is a guest in my country. But then again, the aphid that nearly destroyed France's entire wine industry did come from North America. And, I have tasted French brandy. It is much better than this dishwater the hotel calls brandy.

Holding his glass up, as if offering a toast, he says, "I will ask my father to send a case in the next diplomatic pouch."

"It must be a very large pouch."

"You would be surprised. Speaking of diplomacy, I sent a dispatch to Ambassador Jules Patenôtre vis-à-vis the disposition of Mr. Dean's remains."

"And?"

"I'm informed that since he has been returned to his home and properly interned, France considers that issue at an end."

"Good," I say as the waiter returns with an offer of more brandy. "No, thank you, I'll be down momentarily. Please have the charges available." After Delacroix's comment, there's no way I'm about to have more of the hotel's third-rate imitation.

"Mr. Myer, please, I insist, allow me."

"Next time, possibly over a dinner accompanied by a bottle of your fine *diplomatic* brandy."

"It's settled."

"Before I take my leave, I have a request concerning Mr. Dean's death."

"Yes."

"It would help if we could show the court a death certificate to establish the girls are orphans."

"Paris is in *Île-de-France*, a region known to be a stickler for formality. Because the body was spirited away without an autopsy, there's no certificate of death—*acte de décès.*"

"Is there anything we can do?"

"I will bring your request to the attention of my superiors. I'm sorry, there's nothing more I can do."

"Thank you, captain. I couldn't ask for more."

"*Pas de problème*, however, the issue of the unlawful removal of the children remains to be settled."

"Do you think any court in the United States will allow any country, even an ally as close as France, to take two of our citizens from our hands for anything less than a capital offense?"

"It matters not what I believe. I have my orders, which I shall obey. I can't do otherwise."

"I understand. In the meantime, I'll keep you informed of my intended court actions, but I will not share with you or your government my strategy to quash your government's demand." Our exchange contains none of the animosity I felt at our first meeting.

"*Merci beaucoup*, Mr. Myer. I will accord you the same courtesy. As soon as I receive word about the death certificate, I will advise you. If there's a change in my orders, I will inform you before taking action."

THE NEXT DAY I TRAVEL TO THE FAIRFIELD County Courthouse, where I find an inadequate law library. The out-of-date files are more of a hindrance than a help. About to give up and endure a trip to the state capital where there are complete records of recent decisions, a matronly woman passes the open door, then returns and enters. I introduce myself. She identifies herself as the chief clerk and asks what I'm researching. When I tell her adoption, she says, "Come with me, young man," smiles, and turns away.

I've been an attorney long enough to know when a clerk of the court, especially the chief clerk, tells you to come along, you smile and say, "Yes, ma'am."

She leads me downstairs to a room with rows of shelves filled with boxes, cleaning supplies, and old and broken furniture—a storage room. Taking a brass key from a pocket, she unlocks and opens another door into a well-stocked law library. I can't believe the sight.

"I'm confused."

"Young lawyers and a few other visitors tend to steal the volumes, so we keep this locked. Only the judge and the clerks have a key."

"I'm honored, ma'am."

"Make sure you lock the door behind you and bring me the key when you leave." She smiles and adds, "You can rest assured, young man, I will check to make sure everything has been left intact."

I spend several hours poring over Connecticut's adoption laws and case decisions related to the subject. The pronouncements are straightforward; any kin to an orphaned child is granted first and almost exclusive rights to custody, a usual occurrence in adoption cases. Based on my talks with Katie and Ada Mae, I'm certain they have no living relatives. One precedent does give me cause for concern, one that could well be an insurmountable obstacle to Lura's adoption of the girls. I take a great many notes before returning the key to the clerk and expressing my gratitude for her kindness.

Before starting back to Ridgefield, I decide to discuss the disturbing decision with Louis Brandeis. I send him a telegram with this information and the results of my meeting with Captain Delacroix. I ask him to come to Ridgefield to discuss strategy and meet Delacroix.

Reaching Grisham Manor well into the night, all seem to be asleep. While I'm unhitching the horse from the cabriolet, Earl appears. Wearing a threadbare housecoat over his nightclothes, and with heavy work boots on, he makes an incongruous image. He reaches for the horse's halter as I make a pretense of refusing his help.

"Mr. Myer, you must be exhausted, so let's not argue, sir. You go on up and get some sleep. I'll rub the mare down and give her a good helping of oats. She's also tired and needs her rest."

I'M UP EARLY. BEFORE EARL HAS TIME TO REACH the barn and object to my attire, I've saddled one of the stallions and am off to Ridgefield. The hotel dining room is open, and after a splendid breakfast of ham, poached eggs, and fresh hot biscuits, I visit the telegraph office and get another message off to Brandeis.

Returning to the hotel, I leave a note at the front desk for Captain Delacroix advising him that I'll be on the balcony should he find a few minutes to spare. The waiter brings coffee as I study my notes on Connecticut's adoption laws and that one damnable case decision. My second cup has grown cold by the time Delacroix and the waiter appear at my table. After ordering his meal, Delacroix inquires as to what he might do for me. I tell him about the potentially damaging case decision and my hope to overcome it. He agrees it could be troublesome but offers his wishes for a successful conclusion.

After returning to Grisham Manor and stabling the stallion, Earl fetches me to Lura's office, which he refers to as "Mr. George's study." Though I know perfectly well where the study is, I wait for the always proper Earl to escort me. He directs me to one of two deep and well-aged leather chairs in front of a dark desk and goes to fetch Lura. The exquisitely carved desk is mahogany with ornate corner pieces supporting a marble top. The depth looks to be normal-sized, maybe twenty inches, while the width is well beyond what I'd consider normal. It must be over six feet.

My mind leaves the desk, replaced by an image of Lura. I'm growing more and more enchanted with her, constantly looking forward to our meetings. Who am I kidding? I'm falling in love with this willful, exasperatingly wonderful woman.

The chair's leather is worn as smooth as silk. I imagine Lura's skin smoother than the finest Chinese silk. I close my eyes and picture her sitting on my lap as I kiss her lovely lips. My reverie is brought to an abrupt halt when I contemplate my brother doing what I'm imagining. The impropriety of my feelings—desire—brings me back to reality. Forcing myself to stop fantasizing about her, I take in the room as if seeing it for the first time. The desk, the walls, even the chair legs, appear to be cut from the same mahogany. I don't recall the last time I sat in such a comfortable and luxurious chair. This isn't strong enough to quell my thoughts of her, there, in my arms, and miracle of miracles, she's returning my embrace—caresses—with a hunger I've never known.

Lura walks in, and my dream world collapses in mortification. I picture her seeing into my mind, able to see the foulness of my imaginary love affair. I'm mistaken and have escaped detection, for she smiles and hands me a snifter of brandy, warmed. A sip proves much, much better than that served at the hotel. I start to stand, but she waves me down and reaches for a model of an early Pullman car. She flips the roof back, opening it, exposing the contents—cigars.

"When George Pullman approached my father about coupling his cars to our trains, he gave Father this box as a gift. They both loved a good cigar. Father passed the habit on to me." She takes a cigar, cuts its tip, lights it, and hands it to me as if we're at a gentlemen's club. She repeats the process, keeping the fresh cigar in her mouth, smirking. "What?" she asks and without waiting for an answer, takes a snifter in her hand and sits in the other easy chair.

Caught unawares, I mumble "Not very ladylike," and immediately realize I've made a mistake and take a sip of brandy. The comment doesn't help me. Damn.

"This is my home, my brandy, my cigars, and I don't give a whit if you find my behavior unladylike or not."

Hoping to change the subject, I ask what she thinks about the Pullman Strike that began in Chicago the previous May.

"Railroads west of Chicago lost a great deal, and the deaths and injuries were unnecessary. We were fortunate." She takes a swallow of brandy, followed by a drag on her cigar. "The strike didn't create any undue hardship on my rail lines." After another pull on her cigar, she adds, "I'm not interested in chitchat. We're here to discuss the girls' future. Tell me, what have you learned?"

"We have to prove that the girls have no living relatives before your petition to adopt can be settled."

"How?"

"I'll begin by interviewing the girls."

"I've already talked to them. There are no relatives."

"I don't doubt you or the girls, but we must document all our efforts. There's always the chance an aunt, an uncle, or some other distant relative exists."

"How can that be?"

"I'm a perfect example. Not even Walter's father knew of my existence."

"Oh, my Lord," Lura sits back with a sigh. *Lord* seems to linger in the air—slurred. Has she already had a snifter or two of the brandy?

"What if there's someone? What can we do? I can't lose the girls. I've already lost so much."

Lura's love for the girls consumes her. I can see it and hear it whenever she's around them or talking about them. Her fear of losing them, so strong, is palpable. I'm filled with a sensation of apprehension. I've begun to share her feelings so I try to offer her relief—hope.

"It's unlikely there are any relatives, but we have to do what we can to either find them or prove none exists. We have no choice."

"Why not?"

"It's a requirement of law in a civil action—adoption is civil."

"I know. Don't treat me like a child. Go on."

"We must prove we've investigated sufficiently to obtain the necessary information. It's called due diligence."

"How do we do that?"

"Hire detectives."

"Maybe I should take the girls and leave the country."

From her tone, and the look on her face, this isn't the first time this idea has crossed her mind. I understand and want to satisfy her every wish. As her lawyer, I cannot—will not—allow my emotions to cloud my judgment.

"That would fail, and you would lose the girls."

"If I were to go somewhere like Australia, no one would ever know. I have more than enough money to start a new life."

"Lura, it might be conceivable, but just because you have a wish and the means to make it possible, doesn't mean it will come true."

She might be able to run, but life as she knows it would be destroyed—gone forever—with no way back. Leaving America might even hasten her losing the children. She might even lose her freedom. With her money and the notoriety, she wouldn't be able to hide anywhere for long. Politics would determine the outcome. Neither English speaking Australia nor Britain would defy French claims, not now when both are currying favor with her. Lura's greatest chance of success lies here in America.

"You can't think that way, nor can you say anything like that ever again. If you do, it could be used against you in court."

"You're my lawyer. I can say anything I want to you."

"To a degree that's true, but there are exceptions, and we must prepare. When the adoption petition is heard, you will testify. If there's a challenge, the other party's attorney will examine you, question you under oath. You can't lie."

"Why would you suggest such a thing?"

There she goes again, interrupting when I'm trying to explain the process. Why must every conversation end in a quarrel? If it were anyone but her, I would have already gone back to New York.

"I'm not suggesting you would be less than truthful. But you must follow my advice."

"Damn you."

She jumps out of her chair and slams her glass down so hard it breaks. "I'll never take orders from you. How dare you. This is my—"

Before she can finish, I'm on my feet. The difference is I set my glass down without breaking it and put my cigar in an ashtray.

"I'm your lawyer." I realize I'm shouting, but I can't stop. "You have to allow me to do my job."

We're both shouting now and without bothering to knock, Earl's there, in the room, between us.

"Missy Lura?" Concern apparent in his voice.

She almost runs into his arms before she catches herself. Earl repeats his question, more calmly than the first time, but she stomps around him and storms out, her eyes ablaze.

Earl silently picks up the broken snifter carefully, piece by piece. Once he fills his left hand with broken glass, he walks silently to the door and leaves. He's back within minutes with a broom and bucket. Remaining silent, he cleans the remnants of Lura's glass and cigar from the carpet. Once the mess is cleared away, he moves to the door, opens it, and turns to me.

"You must forgive her." He closes the door behind him.

I would have felt less shame if he had rebuked me for upsetting her. I sit in silence for I don't know how long. Shadows travel across the still room as the sun's light sinks in the West. Have I destroyed any feelings she may have had for me? I stare at the ashtray and the remnants of my long-dead cigar until I doze.

When I awake, it's dark. A lamp glows dimly on the desk. Lura is sitting in the other chair, her eyes red. Has she been crying? We first talked when I awoke on the ship with her sitting at my side. She wasn't crying then. Was that when I fell in love with her?

I move to her. Getting to my knees, I take her hands in mine.

"Please, forgive me. You know how I feel about you."

"You mustn't say things like that."

"I didn't mean you should obey me. It was wrong—stupid."

"That isn't what I meant. You mustn't . . . I'm . . . I'm not . . . ready." She pulls her hands from mine and stands.

Rising with her, I take her in my arms. She pulls away and then touches my face. After a moment, she sobs quietly and flees the room.

AFTER BREAKFAST, ALONE, I GO TO THE STABLES TO saddle the stallion. Earl's there with the girls. They are excited because he's going to give them a riding lesson. Before I can saddle the horse, he tells me Lura wants me to wait a few minutes.

"She wants to ride to town with you," he says.

Lura joins me as soon as I have the cabriolet ready. When we get to the end of the drive, she tells me to take the turn away from town.

"I want to finish our conversation in private."

I reach for her hand. She hesitates as if to refuse my entreaty, but allows me to touch her. We ride in silence for several minutes. I can't continue the pretense.

"Lura, oh, Lura, last night was . . ."

She pulls her hand away from mine.

"Please, Joseph. I wish to finish our conversation without allowing inappropriate feelings to get in the way."

"I disagree our feelings were . . . are . . . appropriate."

"Can we finish our conversation?" she says, her voice apologetic, tender.

"If you tell Emily—anyone—you're thinking about taking the girls to Australia, anything that could jeopardize the adoption, you could be asked a direct question in court. You would have to answer it."

"I understand."

"Except for me, you must not discuss the adoption with anyone."

"What of the girls?"

"I'll represent them if they want to be adopted by you."

"They do."

"I'll have to be the judge of that once I talk with them."

She swallows audibly, obviously upset, but I adopt a professional tone because it's crucial she understands the importance of the girls' decision.

"I have to ask the girls many things. Some of what they say, I might not be able to discuss with you. You must trust me."

"I do," she concedes.

"It's in the best interests of you and the girls."

"I know, but how can I not talk with the girls? I love them. For God's sake, they live in my house."

"Talk to them, care for them, tell them what we're doing for them."

She smiles, tries to hide it by looking away. Then I realize I said it again. *We*.

"I don't deny caring for you," she says, looking away, "but it's too soon."

I want nothing more than to pull off the road and take her into my arms, hold her, kiss her. She's driving me crazy with longing, desire, to marry her and spend the rest of my life making her and the girls happy. Why can't she accept that?

Instead, I honor her wishes and return the conversation to safer ground.

"Talk with Katie and Ada Mae as much as you

like and about anything you wish, except the adoption. When the four of us are together, we can talk openly. Our conversations, while I represent the three of you, are protected, to a degree, by the attorney-client privilege. However, we must be careful. Privilege doesn't apply when I'm not acting as your attorney."

"What do you mean?"

"Let's say, for example, Louis and Giovanni are discussing the sale of your holdings, and I'm with them. If you're there, and we slip into talk of the adoption, the privilege is waived. Any of us can be questioned about our conversation." Continuing to play the role of a lawyer while explaining these issues is nigh onto impossible with my feelings for her running a race with my thoughts of duty. How can I control my thoughts when she is sitting next to me, our bodies touching?

"I can't stand it any longer. I love you, and you love me."

"Joseph, dear Joseph. Whatever can I . . . it's hopeless."

"Marry me."

"Marry you? Are you out of your mind?"

She reaches over and pulls the reins from my hands and brings the carriage to a stop.

"Get out."

"What?"

"Get out."

She shoves me, and I get off the carriage,

stupefied. Grabbing the buggy whip, she gives the horse a flick, and the carriage pulls away, leaving me there, in the dust alongside the road.

The walk back to Grisham Manor takes the better part of an hour.

TWENTY-FOUR

JOSEPH MYER

Tired from my unexpected—and unwanted—morning walk, I bathe and take a short nap before hearing a knock at my bedroom door. Can it be Lura? Please let it be her. It's not; it's Earl. He announces it's time for my chat with the girls.

I'm seated at the desk in George's study when Katie arrives. She's not her usual self. She even knocks on the open door. When I tell her to come in, she doesn't run and hug me. She stands rigid, arms locked tight across her chest.

"Miss Lura says I have to talk to you and answer your questions, even if I don't want to," she says in a shrill voice and then, in a whisper, asks, "Is that true?"

I get up from behind the desk and walk to her.

"It'll be okay," I say, hoping to overcome her

reluctance. She backs away, and I stop. I don't wish to upset her any further.

"Why can't Miss Lura or Ada Mae be with me?"

"You know Miss Lura wants to adopt you and Ada Mae." I must get her talking, relaxed.

"So?"

"Can you tell me what adoption means to you?"

"It means we get to stay with Miss Lura, and she'll be our mama."

"That's right, Katie, but it's more complicated than staying with Miss Lura."

"I know. We'll be Miss Lura's children, but Mama and Papa will always be our mama and papa. We can love them and Miss Lura."

"There is a great deal grown-up people must do before they can adopt a child."

She fidgets. Her face contorts so much, her mouth twists into a grotesquely shaped smile, and her eyebrows almost come together. She looks back towards the door, her body shaking. She's on the verge of running. Can I stop her?

"I want Miss Lura," she yelps.

"I'm sorry. I'll go and get her."

The child is in tears, and I realize I've been speaking to her as if she's an adult, as if I were cross-examining a witness. My God. I rush to the great room and find Lura sitting in a straight-back chair under a portrait of her father and mother. She rises as soon as she sees my expression.

"I knew it."

She pushes by and rushes, with me at her heels, to the study.

"Oh, darling."

Sobbing, Katie throws herself into Lura's arms, whose look sends shivers down my spine.

"Leave us alone," she hisses with a terrifying finality that makes me shudder.

She closes her eyes, lips tight. I can't go on. All I can do is retreat to the great room where Earl, unaware of my turmoil, offers me an afternoon repast. I have no appetite, but to avoid hurting anyone else's feelings, I accept his offer, even though I don't touch the pastries and coffee proffered by the kindly man.

Ada Mae storms into the room and comes right at me.

"Why did you make Katie cry?" I cringe at her fierceness. She's a brave girl challenging a grown-up to tell her what he did to upset her sister.

"I didn't mean to."

"Are you sorry?"

My God. A twelve-year-old girl is interrogating me.

"Yes, I am."

She gets out of her chair, walks around the table, and takes my hand.

"You need to tell her you're sorry."

She tugs on me until I'm standing and then leads me across the room. I'm not resisting, but she doesn't release my hand, not for a second. At the door to the study, I remember Lura's hissed command. I freeze mid-step.

"Miss Lura told me to leave. She doesn't want me in there. She'll be mad."

"It's alright," Ada Mae says and opens the door. "You're with me."

Lura looks up, her eyes hard as she fixes me with a cold stare. When she sees Ada Mae, leading me by the hand, she gives the child a quizzical look.

"Ada Mae?"

"Joseph's sorry he made Katie cry. He wants to tell her." She pulls me close to Katie, takes her sister's hand, and joins our hands together. "Tell Joseph you forgive him."

"No! I won't. He scared me. I hate him," she says and jerks away.

I reach out to her. She rewards me with a kick to my shin. It doesn't hurt, but the shock of it does. Her behavior is unlike anything I've seen from her. Speechless, I step back to the doorway, arms raised. I want to hide.

"No, no, you don't," Ada Mae yells and grabs her sister.

Lura drops to her knees and envelops the girls in her arms. Shushing them, she rocks back and forth. After a moment, she turns toward me. The look on her face tells me she would crush me in her bare hands if they weren't locked in the embrace of the girls. Legs shaking, heart hammering, I drop to my knees, and I try to wrap my arms around all three.

Katie mumbles something through her tears. It's all I can do to keep from weeping.

"Let me go," she snaps. "You scared me. I'm mad at you and Ada Mae for saying I have to forgive you. I don't forgive you. I hate you." Arms tight across her chest, face red, she shakes with rage.

"It's no wonder you frightened the poor child." Perhaps to reduce the tension by changing the subject, Lura says, "This room is dark and intimidating. You might have opened the curtains and let a little sunlight brighten it up." Lura's words, serious though they are, are softened by the forgiveness I see in her gentle smile and the relaxing of her gaze. She pulls the heavy drapes open, allowing the light to stream in. She's right. The room is no longer hostile, but rather cheery, a welcome haven. Katie reacts to the warmth, and to Lura, who wraps her arms around the child. The change in Katie isn't sudden but evolves as her arms loosen, and she returns Lura's embrace. As the shaking dissipates, the color of her face lightens and returns to normal.

"I'm sorry I said mean things," she mumbles.

Lura asks—orders might be a better word—Ada Mae and me to leave. It's back to the dining room where I'm in no mood to eat. Ada Mae wolfs down several molasses cookies and a glass of milk and surprises me with a pat on my shoulder.

"Don't worry, Joseph," she says when she's done. "Katie's a brat. She doesn't hate you."

She kisses me on the cheek. I can't help tearing

up. Acting more like my big sister than the child she is, she dabs the tears away with her napkin.

"It's okay. It's okay."

Lura walks in with Katie in tow, now all smiles.

"Girls," she says. "Cook is making a batch of blueberry scones. If you hurry, you should be in time for some hot and fresh from the oven."

"Yes," they answer in unison and are up and out the door before she finishes.

"You can talk with the girls tomorrow," Lura says to me coldly. "I'll have them ready for you."

LURA MYER

I join the girls in the kitchen. Cook has a platter of steaming scones on the breakfast table. The girls are barely able to contain their enthusiasm as she pours cold milk into tall glasses.

"Cook, please bring a glass for me," I say as I slide in next to Katie.

Both girls giggle when I take a big gulp and milk dribbles down the sides of my mouth.

"Miss Lura always does that when she has a glass of milk and eats my scones," Cook says through a giant smile.

I can't think of a better—safer—place to have a serious conversation with the girls; one we should have had long before subjecting them to Joseph's questioning. I mouth a silent request for Cook to give us some privacy.

"I must dig up some ginger root," she says. "Nothing better than fresh ginger to put the snap in my gingersnaps." The girls want to help her.

"No, stay here," I say, sharper than necessary."I have something to say to you."

Disappointed, but curious, they sit. After all, hot blueberry scones and milk are quite the consolation.

"If you truly want me to adopt you, you must talk to Joseph and answer his questions." From their reactions—they stop eating and put their milk down—I have their attention.

"Joseph will ask a judge to let me adopt you."

"Why does a judge get to say if you can adopt us?" asks Ada Mae, another question Joseph and I should have answered long before.

"The judge will ask questions, maybe many questions. Joseph's job is to ask you the same questions first. That's why he tried to talk to Katie. He didn't do it very well. He doesn't understand girls, so we have to excuse him."

Katie's still angry and voices her objection to meeting with him. "I won't," she shouts, "I won't. You can't make me," shouting even louder as she stands and starts to move away.

"Sit down, and don't say another word." I've had all I can take of her hostile behavior for one day. "You will do as I say, or you can leave now and find another home." My reaction is stronger than necessary. I flush with the shame of it, but it brings an end to her rebelliousness, at least what I can see, and she grudgingly agrees to forgive Joseph.

"If Joseph asks you a question you don't understand or frightens you, tell him."

JOSEPH MYER

Shortly before sunset, Lura and I walk in the garden. She holds my arm as we stroll. She's brighter and more talkative than usual, whereas I find myself struggling for words. She goes on and on about her conversation with the girls as her touch sends tremors that add to the pounding in my heart. I assure her my next meeting with Katie will be more productive than the fiasco earlier in the day, but mostly, I'm thankful for the slight breeze because it halts what could have been the embarrassment of visibly damp underarms. It's a joy being near her. How can she not feel this?

A flock of birds darkens the sky in ever-changing billows as if a sign from God.

"Look," I say, pointing.

"Those damnable birds are no friends of mine. Besides their raucous screeching, they destroy the apples and peaches in our orchards. Unless we are sharp-eyed and pick the fruit before ripe, we lose them to those filthy creatures." Lura's response takes me by surprise.

"Oh," is all I can muster.

"You didn't know. After all, you are a city boy," she says with a teasing laugh and a toss of her head.

Her warmth heightens my feelings for her. Searching for a way out of this predicament—this cornucopia of hope, dreams—I look for an escape. What could be a sanctuary appears as if by magic. I spy an ancient weeping willow with an opening trimmed to form an arch over the airy inner area. In the roomy space beneath the overhead branches sits a bench, perfect for a couple. I seize the opportunity to guide Lura toward this relaxed setting and to cool my passion by discussing the reason—really an excuse—for inviting her to walk in the garden.

"Shall we sit and deliberate our next steps?"

Lura agrees, and I lead her to the area, which is larger and more secluded than I had imagined. Turning, I gaze out the opening at a dazzling view of the fast-approaching sunset. The beauty freezes me in time.

"Father made the bench for Mother." Pointing toward the sun, she says, "They often came here, held hands, and watched the sunset before dinner."

"It's beautiful."

I turn and look into her eyes.

"He must have loved her greatly."

"He did," her voice soft, choked. "Dinner often waited until after their sunset."

Tears flow, and not just hers. I pull her close, and she rests her head against my shoulder. We remain thus for a moment, enjoying the closeness, before separating in self-conscious silence.

I follow her to the bench. As we sit, our hips

touch. We almost jump apart. Laughing, we exchange silly grins.

"Pardon me," she says with a smile.

The air is so charged that I launch into talk of the adoption to stay sane. "It's time to ask the court to appoint me as the girls' attorney. It shouldn't be a problem. If it becomes one, I'll ask Louis to replace me and argue the case. Regardless, we'll protect the girls' rights."

"I'm concerned about you," she says as she clutches at my arm. She's either nervous, frightened, agitated, or all three.

"Me?"

"You've been away from New York for over a month."

I'm stunned, thinking she is sending me away now, after everything we've been through, but it's as if she senses the direction of my thoughts. She looks me in the eye.

"You can't spend all your time here. You have to think about your business, your other clients."

I'm so relieved, I grin. I'm flattered Lura's concerned about me. I'm more than flattered. I want to take her in my arms; however, some sense of propriety tells me she wouldn't have it—not now. Instead, I slide closer, and hips touching, put my hand on her arm. I experience the oddest clench in my stomach, a sensation I've not felt since my youth. I want to kiss my brother's widow, but as the thought of Walter enters my mind, my body retreats of its own accord, creating an invisible barrier between us.

"Oh, Joseph," she sighs and looks away, "it's more than concern for your business."

"What then?"

"I was afraid if we remained in New York, my impatience—obsession—with the adoption would drive you away. Here, at Grisham Manor, getting to know the girls . . . I knew . . . hoped . . . by coming here to Connecticut, you would be far less likely to—"

"Lura," I whisper. I want to say I would never abandon her, but no words come. It's as if I've forgotten how to breathe. I keep thinking soon, very soon, I'll take a breath and say the words, but no breath comes.

"Oh, look," she says, breaking the awkward silence, pointing at the gorgeous, churning sunset.

I mutter in agreement and can't even do that right as I stumble over the words. What's wrong with me?

"Maybe we should talk about the girls," she says, coming to my rescue.

"I've hired detectives to conduct the search. As far as they know, we want to find the family. They'll search for any living relatives. That will help us provide the court with the proof necessary to support your request for adoption."

"How long will it take?"

She's disappointed. Her dissatisfaction pricks at my heart, much the same as a cactus spine would bite a finger. Not serious, but how many such wounds can a heart tolerate?

"As long as there are leads to follow." I take a breath now that I can breathe. "We know where Mr. Dean lived when his wife died. The detectives will interview neighbors to see if they can locate anyone who knew them, where they were married, where they were born."

"Why?"

"There's a great deal to be learned, which may show whether other children were born to either of their parents. Marriages, though not always documented, can identify friends and family members who, in turn, can lead to other sources of information."

"What if there's a sister, a brother unknown?" followed by a whispered, "such as yourself."

"Let's wait and see. It can be time-consuming, go in many directions, and become expensive."

"I'm not concerned with costs, only that we satisfy the courts. I hope they find nothing."

"Remember, we have to be open-minded. That's why the detectives only know I want the relatives located. They don't need to know anything else. However, being detectives, I'd be surprised if they haven't already realized that the search is part of an adoption investigation."

"How soon will we know something—anything?"

"Within days. They send me a telegram every time they find or exhaust a lead, no matter how large or small."

"When do you expect a report?"

"I imagine there'll be one waiting in the morning."

Afraid desire will overcome reason, I use the excuse that it's gotten full dark and quite chilly to suggest we return to the manor house.

LURA MYER

"My, but this is a hearty breakfast. Were you expecting one of Father's railroad men?" I say when Cook places two plates on the table, but across from where I sit. A large Delmonico steak covers one, the other with four fried eggs and potatoes. The ensemble is complete when she returns with biscuits, a bowl of blackberries, and a steaming cup of coffee.

"Mr. Myer usually arrives early, as your father did, with a large appetite. He's late today."

The last time Cook mentioned Father and late in the same sentence was the day he died. She must have the same thought, for the look on her face mirrors the feeling I experience.

"Where's my coffee?" Joseph bursts in before either of us have a chance to speak.

"Cook, what have you done? You've allowed Lura to abscond with my breakfast," he says with a roar.

She laughs and gives him a gentle slap on the arm. Cook has taken a liking to him, and he to her.

"Take mine. It's too much for me," I say.

Without a word, he sits down and pulls the plates to him and then reaches for my coffee.

"You go too far, Mr. Myer. Taking food from my mouth is one thing, but how dare you presume my coffee is fair game. How dare you," I say in mock anger.

As I pull my cup away from his grasping hand, Cook places a mug before him. Smiling, he grips it, takes a swallow, turns, and congratulates her on making the finest coffee in Connecticut.

"Only Connecticut? What of New York?" She laughs as she moves to her stove and cracks a pair of eggs for me.

Joseph's chatty with Cook, polite to me. Where is the passion I saw in him last night? Was what I felt—what I thought we shared—my imagination? No. It was real.

"Cook, would you be so kind as to ask Earl to hitch the Tilbury for me. I wish to go into town."

"Yes, Miss Lura."

"Joseph, I have business in town. Would it be an inconvenience if I asked you to drive me?"

Joseph is quiet, subdued, during the ride. With him driving, I have the opportunity to study him. I see more of Walter in him each day. It's a shame the two never met. They would have liked each other. Arriving in town, and for reasons I don't understand, I'm disappointed the ride is over so soon.

I wait in the carriage for Joseph to return. When he comes out of the telegraph office, he stops, turns, and looks down. It looks as if he's either shaking his head or talking with someone. I decide he's talking to himself as his head continues shaking as he steps down from the sidewalk. He stops next to the carriage. He must be troubled.

"What's wrong?"

"Let's see Emily first. There is a problem I need to think over. Do you mind?"

"No, not at all. Let's see what's going on with Emily at the mercantile." I do mind, but I have an obligation to him as my attorney to let him do his job. During the short ride, Joseph's silent.

Emily is hustling and bustling about the store with an air of confidence. The workers are comfortable around her, yet respectful and hard-working. She wastes no time or effort. "Lura, it's wonderful to see you. Joseph, you look upset." It's obvious; he's forcing a strained smile in a futile attempt to hide the frown he has worn since leaving the telegraph office.

"You're very perceptive, Emily. I have a matter that gives me cause for concern. Do you have a room where I could be alone for a few minutes?"

"Let me show you the way to my office. You can use it as long as necessary. No one will bother you."

After depositing Joseph in her office, Emily returns. "Is he always this somber?"

"No. It has to with a telegraph from the detectives in Boston. I don't know what to make of it."

"If he needs time to be alone, why don't you and

263

I go to the hotel? We should be in time for tea." Emily has always been sensible.

"That sounds much more pleasant than waiting around here. It will give us a chance to visit, and I want your advice about some outfits for the girls."

"Good." When we reach the door, I hesitate and start to turn back.

"Lura dear, if you wait here, you'll stew until you interrupt Joseph." She looks toward the office door and lets out a sigh. "You can't do any good waiting and worrying. Besides, we can see the front of the store from the hotel."

I grudgingly agree.

We find Captain Delacroix relaxing on the hotel veranda. He comes to attention and bows as Emily and I climb the few steps to the porch. "Good afternoon, Mrs. Myer. It is a pleasure to see you."

"And you, sir." I'm not in the mood for genteel conversation, but good manners require an introduction. "Emily, this is Captain Julien Delacroix of the French Army. He is the military attorney whose duty is to prevent my adoption of Katie and Ada Mae by forcing me to return them to France."

I can't keep my eyes from wandering to the front of Emily's store. I want to know what has happened, and I do not want to wait one minute longer.

"Mademoiselle, please do not portray me as such an ogre to your charming friend. I'm but a simple soldier trying to do his duty."

"My dear Captain, I understand your position,

and outside of the political situation into which I've drawn you, Joseph speaks highly of you. Please accept my apology for speaking disparagingly of your position. Allow me to begin again."

"*Très certainement, Mademoiselle.*"

"Captain, may I present Miss Emily Bartolini. Emily and I have been friends our entire lives."

"*C'est un honneur*, Miss Bartolini."

"You must forgive me, Captain. I don't speak French."

"My apologies. No insult meant."

I can see Emily is taken with the handsome captain as she says, "None taken, Captain." I don't have time for her flirtatiousness.

"Would you ladies do me the honor of joining a lonely soldier for tea?"

"We came here to enjoy the tea. Having you join us will only increase our pleasure."

"Captain Delacroix, would you be so kind as to fetch the waiter and order tea? I wish to remain here on the veranda." Emily answers before I get the chance.

My Lord, what has come over these two? They have exceeded all boundaries of good taste within mere moments of meeting. Am I being old fashioned?

Tea is very pleasant for Emily and Delacroix. They keep up a lively conversation while I worry about Joseph and the unknown—certainly unwelcome—news he carries.

Before the tea has time to turn cold, a somber Joseph joins us. "The news I have is very disturbing."

"What is it?" I'm thunderstruck. Once again, I find myself crushing my pendant. When did I start calling it my pendant?

"We should discuss this in private."

"I agree."

Emily and Delacroix stand, offer apologies, and take their leave.

"What is it?" I grab Joseph by both arms. I'm creating a scene, but I'm beyond caring. "Tell me now." He looks around to make sure no one is near enough to overhear our conversation.

"I don't know how to tell you this."

"For Lord's sake, Joseph."

He takes a deep breath.

"I've hired detectives in Boston to search for members of the Dean family. At first, I wanted to use Pinkertons from New York, detectives with whom I've worked within the past, and for whom I have the greatest respect. I discussed this with Brandeis. He suggested that detectives in Boston would have a greater chance."

"What difference does it make where the detectives come from?"

"It shouldn't make any difference, but I fear it did."

"Say it, for God's sake."

"Please, you're causing a scene. People are staring."

"Tell me before I scream." I pound my fists on

his chest. I'm beyond caring what others may think. I must know. I must.

"The detectives may have connections to the Irish Mob."

His words slowly sink in. I sense pain in my hand and realize I'm squeezing my pendant again.

"The report claims they have found a half-sister of Francis Dean and she's demanding access to, and custody of, the girls."

"No." I feel burning in my eyes and fight back the tears that want to flow. "Oh, Lord. I can't suffer another loss of this magnitude. It has to be a mistake."

"I don't know if there's a mistake or not. My concern is that the Irish Mob learned of my investigation."

"I ask again, Joseph, what concerns do you harbor about the Irish Mob and the search for Mr. Dean's relatives?"

"I fear that relatives, real or pretend, will come forward and demand custody of the girls. Claims are likely because of your connection to Katie and Ada Mae. These people may want your money."

First the French officials, now these charlatans. How many more will I have to pay off—bribe? "How much?"

"No one has asked for money so far."

"How many are claiming to be related to Mr. Dean?"

"So far, only one."

"What do we know of her?"

"She claims to be Mr. Dean's illegitimate half-sister, born to his father's mistress."

"That sounds familiar, doesn't it?"

As soon as the words are out of my mouth, Joseph's face flushes. I can see I've embarrassed him.

"I didn't mean it the way it sounded."

Joseph takes my left hand in his; my right clutches the pendant. His hand is warm and strong—a heat I have long missed. I stiffen and start to pull away as a fluttering in my stomach almost over-whelms me. These feelings should not be happening, but I can't help what I have for this man, Walter's brother. I relax and enjoy the warmth of his grip. The tables on either side are no longer occupied. My outburst must have chased them away.

"I know, Lura."

He's quiet for a moment before our eyes meet. Embarrassed, he releases my hand and sits straight.

"I'm sorry."

Although troubled by the news he has delivered, I can't help but feel safe in his company. He's my lawyer. I should be paying attention to the report and how to combat these wild claims. Instead, I'm dreaming of being held in his arms. My God, what's happening to me? I've only been a widow for six months.

"Do you want to hear my plan?" he brings me back to reality.

"Yes."

"First, I'll have the detectives arrange a meeting with the woman. I'll question her myself and get an understanding of what she wants."

"Then?"

"Then I'll do what I should have done from the beginning and bring Detective Donald White of the Pinkertons from New York up to Boston. He can make discreet inquiries without revealing the nature of the investigation while concealing his identity."

"Will you be safe in Boston? I don't want to lose you." What causes me to say these words, words that make my cheeks redden?

"Nor I you." His response brings the same flushing to Joseph's face.

Julien and Emily step onto the veranda. I take a deep breath to compose myself, sit up, and say, "Emily and the captain are about to rejoin us. Is this something we can share with Emily? With Captain Delacroix?"

"That a woman is claiming to be a relative won't remain secret. I see no reason we can't tell them. Captain Delacroix has a legal right to know the status of our investigation. Aside from that, he's an ally, a man we can trust, and in whom we may seek counsel."

Emily looks between Joseph and me. I can tell she senses that more than a conversation between a lawyer and his client has occurred.

"Lura, are you alright?"

"Yes, Joseph has news—a claim—a claim by a

woman who may be a relative."

"Oh, no," Emily gasps.

I invite the two to sit. Joseph explains what he has learned. I tear up, and he takes his handkerchief and dabs at the tears running down my cheek. I take the cloth from his hand, and mine lingers over his. Embarrassed, I sit back and shake my head. Emily gives me an inquiring look. To forestall any awkward questions, I invite the two to dinner.

"Captain, Emily, would you care to join us for dinner tonight at Grisham Manor?"

Neither Emily nor Captain Delacroix seems the least discomforted by my invitation to Grisham Manor on such short notice. Propriety seems unimportant to either.

"I would be delighted if Miss Giovanni would allow me to escort her."

Emily agrees and then surprises me with a knowing smile, followed by a hug and kiss.

My Lord, did I refer to Joseph and me as us?

COOK AND EARL ARE PREPARED FOR THE FOUR OF us. Earl smiles but does not explain when I ask how they knew to prepare such a feast.

Captain Delacroix expresses his concern about the possibility that the woman in Boston might be related to the girls.

"For your sake, Mrs. Myer, I hope it proves to be a false claim. If it's not, and the woman somehow gains custody of the girls, my government will likely withdraw its demand for their return to France."

"That would be of some relief, but what of me? Will France still seek my arrest and extradition?"

"I don't have the authority to answer your question. I believe the longer the question lingers, the less publicity, the greater the chance the demand will die a silent death. That is my fervent wish."

"Captain, we have gone beyond a formal relationship, you are a guest in my home. Would it be so terrible if you were to call me Lura? Mrs. Myer sounds so strict."

"Madame, nothing would please me more, but only if you call me Julien."

I find it difficult to enjoy dinner, even with such splendid guests. Joseph notes my melancholy and attempts to cheer me. "May I play something for you and your guests?"

"Whatever do you mean?"

"Some believe I'm an accomplished pianist. I would be pleased to demonstrate what little skill I have."

Emily claps her hands and says, "Oh, please, Joseph, that would be a delight. Lura, you must insist he play for us."

How can they be so lighthearted when all I can think of is the possibility that I might lose the girls. Before I say something I'll regret, I stop to think. Is my angst merely about the woman in Boston, or is there something else? I suffer some jealousy over the way Emily and Julien seem so enamored with one another. They seem to have forgotten my problem entirely. And what of Joseph? How do I explain what's going on with him? With my feelings? It's difficult for me, but I conceal low spirits considering the joy Joseph wishes to share.

"If you insist, Emily dear, we'll retire to the great room and allow Joseph to regale us with his self-proclaimed talent."

Joseph is a fine pianist. For an hour, he entertains us beginning with "Old Time Religion" and ending with "After the Ball." In between, he throws in a few works of John Phillip Sousa while complaining, "Sousa is a little troublesome without horns."

I'm surprised the fingers of a man who fought so often as a young man and then paid his way through college and law school by fighting in the ring can so gently caress the piano keys.

Captain Delacroix tells us of watching Sousa's band march from the Champs-Elysees to the *Arc de Triomphe.*

Soon it's time for Emily and Julien to return to town. "I'll have Earl bring round the carriage."

While the men exchange a few quiet words, Emily and I go to the cloakroom to retrieve her cape. "Emily, what would your father say? Is it prudent to share a carriage at night without a chaperone?"

"Oh, Lura, whatever do you think will happen? If Julien were to kiss me, I would not be offended. If he doesn't, I might kiss him myself. He's so handsome and such a gentleman. As to Father, I'm fast becoming an old maid. He would encourage me to trap this beautiful man."

"Emily, you're a brazen hussy. He is handsome, isn't he? Be careful darling, you've just met him, and you know what they say about handsome Frenchmen."

"No, I don't. What do people say about handsome Frenchmen?"

"Oh, Emily, I have no idea what they say."

Earl has prepared Captain Delacroix's carriage. He waits under the porte-cochère holding the team ready.

Emily and I exchange kisses, and I hand her over to Julien. After he assists her in the carriage, he turns back. I look at him with what I hope is a stern mother's gaze. Laughing, he takes my hand and twirls me in a circle as if we are dancing. Still laughing, he kisses me on each cheek before saying, "Dearest Lura, Miss Bartolini is in safe hands. You need not fret. It may be that I'm the one in danger."

"Julien, you're incorrigible." As the carriage disappears, Joseph and I stand. I am comfortable and safe with this man.

"I'm tired and will retire once I've tucked the girls in, and we've said our prayers." Taking my hand, Joseph leads me into the house.

Joseph wishes me a good evening and then surprises me by kissing me on the cheek. I feel a rush of warmth throughout my body. Imprudently, I embrace him and kiss his cheek.

Joseph pulls me close and kisses my mouth. For an instant, I return it.

TWENTY-FIVE

JOSEPH MYER

A mere block from the Parker House, my cab stops. When I ask the driver why, he tells me to look out the left side. There, blocking the roadway is a Boston Police paddy wagon. A patrolman is standing at the rear while seven or eight scantily dressed women are cursing as they clamber into the back. Boston's finest and lowest, all within shouting distance. Never fond of Boston, the scene does nothing to improve my opinion.

Three hours shy of noon, and wishing to keep my approach discrete, I hire a carriage to take me to Faneuil Hall. From there, I walk three or four blocks up Union Street to The Bell in Hand Tavern, the oldest operating pub in Boston. It's probably the one place in Boston where I feel at ease. Originally built by a retired town crier, it moved to this red brick building fifty years earlier. Maybe it was the ghost of Daniel Webster, long dead when The Bell moved to Union Street, rumored to have followed Jimmy Wilson's famous ale over to the new location. Whatever the case, it was where I chose to meet.

The two Boston detectives were hired through a fellow law student now practicing in Boston. I see I've made a mistake as the more talkative of them begins his report. He smells of stale whiskey and his words, already difficult to understand through a thick Irish brogue, are slurred. The man's drunk or close to it. His companion is in worse shape.

"Mr. Myer, we chatted up Mr. Dean's neighbors for the information you seek. At first, none could tell us anything about a relative. Then we visited the local pubs and even talked with some of the man's old acquaintances at the Irish Cultural Center. Still no luck in finding a relative."

"Why did you go to the pubs and the Irish Cultural Center?"

"Considering the line of work Mr. Dean was in, we figured some of his old cronies might have something for us."

"Did you get anything from his old cronies, all thieves and murderers, I imagine?"

"Mr. Myer, we're Irish ourselves. These are all honorable men. We got nothing at first. But then I had an inspiration. I offered a reward for anyone leading me to a relative of his. It worked. Paddy O'Toole—he owns O'Toole's Tavern—sent for me." He pauses to drain half a glass of ale. "He told me that for fifty dollars, he would introduce me to Francis Dean's half-sister, Mary McCarthy. So I gives him the fifty."

"And?"

"'Why, he calls his barmaid over and asks her, 'Mary, do you know Francis Dean?'"

"'She says to me, she does, 'Why, Francis Dean's my brother, only he don't know it.'"

I'm skeptical of the truth in their report and in what Miss McCarthy is claiming. I'm not sure how to proceed, but I'm finished with these two drunken fools. "Thank you for your service. I don't need anything else from you."

"Seeing as how we found the lady, would you be considering a bonus for a job well done?"

"Present your invoice for services rendered, and I'll entertain a suitable sum." I doubt they deserve a penny, but I'm in no mood to start a disturbance.

The two are all smiles as they order another round of whiskeys. I decline their invitation to join them.

The following day, I meet with the Pinkerton Detectives at the Parker House. This meeting is more congenial as we enjoy coffee along with the hotel's world-famous Parker House Chocolate Cream Pie.

"Mr. Myer, we've interviewed Miss Mary McCarthy, and there's nothing to make us believe she's related to Mr. Francis Dean."

"Why not?"

"She claims she's the product of a liaison between Mr. Dean's father, Patrick Dean, and her mother."

"Such liaisons are not all that uncommon. Give me a summary of what you've learned."

Detective White hands me a written report and begins speaking. "We believe Francis Dean was the son of Patrick and Catherine Dean. We found no birth, death, or burial records for the family. Nor have we found the birth record for Francis Dean. Do you know where he was born?"

"No. I'll try to get you an answer."

"Miss McCarthy says she was born in Worcester in 1864. I sent another detective there to check for any record of her birth."

"I want to interview Miss McCarthy. Arrange a meeting in a public room for tomorrow afternoon. Meanwhile, I want you to contact her neighbors and learn everything you can about her. I want no stone left unturned."

"We'll arrange a meeting. If we run into any difficulties—"

"If I'm not here, I'll be at the courthouse."

THE PINKERTONS ARRANGE THE MEETING. THE female detective, Johanna Guntner, joins me so there can be no claim of misconduct on my part. Mrs. Guntner is an interesting person if only because female detectives are still extremely rare in the profession.

"Mrs. McCarthy, thank you for agreeing to meet with me on such short notice. My name is Joseph Myer, and this is Miss Johanna Guntner. She'll be taking notes. I believe you've already met her."

"Yes, she's the lady who asked me to come here and talk to you about the girls."

"Did she bring you here tonight?"

"Yes, I needed a ride."

"Do you know why I wish to speak with you?"

"Cause I want the girls, my . . . ah . . . ah . . . nieces."

"Can you tell me their names?"

"Ah, ah, Catherine, and Mae . . .?"

"Miss McCarthy, that sounds like a question. Do you know their names?"

"Well, ah, I ain't never rightly met them."

"What is your name?"

"Mary McCarthy."

"How old are you?"

"Thirty."

"Do you have a middle name?"

"Louise. Mary Louise McCarthy."

"Have you ever used any other name?" Before answering, she rubs her hand through the back of her hair. This isn't the only thing I notice. She's biting her lip and staring out the window.

"Whatcha mean? Change my name?"

"Have you ever gone by a different last name?"

"No."

"Was McCarthy your mother's name?"

"No."

"What was your father's name?"

"Patrick Dean." Now she's biting her fingernails. "Can I have a drink or some water?"

"Where did the name McCarthy come from?"

"My mother told me she had to put a father's name down when I was born, so she used McCarthy. Daniel McCarthy was her man then."

"Why didn't she put Patrick Dean on the record?"

Instead of answering me, she comments on how nice my suit looks.

"Did she tell you Patrick Dean was your father?"

Before answering, she once again turns toward the window. Dropping her head forward, she turns in my general direction, balls her right hand into a fist over her mouth, which she bites before mumbling, "Yes."

"Did you ever meet your father?"

"No."

"Did you ever meet Francis?"

"No."

"How do you know Francis was your brother?"

"My mama told me about him a few years ago."

"Where is your mother?"

This time there's no sign of hesitation. "She run off with a whiskey drummer when I was twelve."

"If you've not seen your mother in eighteen years, how is it she told you about your brother Francis Dean a few years ago?"

Caught in a lie, McCarthy's mouth gapes open in silence.

"When did you learn of your brother's death?"

"Mr. O'Toole told me and about the girls."

"How did he know Francis was your brother?"

"Ah . . . ah . . ."

I can't take any more of the woman's lies. It's time to put an end to the farce.

"Mary, O'Toole told you about Francis and then told you to claim to be his half-sister, didn't he?"

The woman's reaction is immediate. Her mouth falls open, but it's hard to see it as she covers her mouth and eyes with her hands. An audible gasp escapes, followed by "No."

"Mary, do you know how I know you're lying?"

"I'm not lying," she whimpers. Hands on her head, elbows close together, she gulps air as she bends over, hiding her face from view.

"Mary, Patrick Dean was born and died in Ireland. He never set foot in America. Your mother never went to Ireland. They never met—never had a child. Do you want to hear more?"

"No."

She begins rocking in the straight-back chair. I can hear her blow out several short breaths while she stares in the direction of the door. After several seconds, she adds, "O'Toole told me to pretend I was their aunt. He told me a rich lady would give me money if I lied."

"How do you know Francis?"

Mary seems to regain her composure as she drops her arms to her lap, raises her head, and looks directly at me. She has become a different woman in a matter of seconds.

"After his wife died, him and me, we had ourselves a fling. It didn't last long. He only wanted to have his way with me. He would get the urge, and we would make a night of it. For a hooligan, he was nice. He loved his daughters mightily."

"Mary, I need you to do something."

"What?"

"I need you to sign a statement that you're not related to Francis Dean or his daughters, Katie and Ada Mae Dean. Can you do that for me?"

"O'Toole will kill me."

"You don't have to mention him in your statement, only that you're not related to the girls and have no claim on them. I won't show the statement to anyone unless you try to make a claim later."

"What do I tell O'Toole?" She starts shaking and rocking again.

"Tell him I called you a liar and threw you out."

She seems to relax and says, "I can do that."

Lura Myer

When Joseph returns from Boston with the good news, I meet him under the portico and impulsively throw my arms around him and squeeze him with all my might. After a second of hesitation, he hugs me back. Our embrace isn't that of brother-and-sister-in-law. Embarrassed, we both back away and talk of nothing important until he retires to his room to freshen up.

When he leaves, it's nigh onto impossible for me to contain the joy I feel. No one is looking. I skip, yes, skip, from the portico to the entrance gate and back. I see Earl in the window with a smile on his face. When I catch his eye, he turns away and disappears.

"UNCLE JOSEPH, WHERE WERE YOU? WE MISSED you."

"I missed you."

Done with the pleasantries, Ada Mae burns to move on to more important matters. "Did you bring us anything, Uncle Joseph?"

"Can you guess what I have in my pocket?"

Now she's ready to pull the pocket from his coat to get at its treasure.

"No, first you must attempt to guess what I have."

"I'm no good at guessing games. Katie, you guess."

"You must give us a hint," Katie, always the analytical one, says.

"You can eat it."

"That's not a good hint."

"Paris."

I know what he holds, but I hold my tongue.

Katie smiles. "I know what it is." Turning to her

sister, she says, "You guess."

Both girls giggle and jump up and down. Katie shouts, "French Chew. It's French Chew." Joseph pulls two small bags from his pocket and hands one to each girl.

"Girls, you must save some. You can't eat it all right now. It will spoil your dinner."

Katie stops and stares at me before saying something that surprises me and fills my heart with joy. "You sound like a mother." I hold my breath and strain to maintain my composure.

Joseph sees my emotional reaction and holds my hand. He saves me with, "I have some French Chew for Miss Lura as well." Releasing me, he makes a flourish with both hands, reaches into the same pocket and brings out one piece of French Chew. As he hands it to me, I want him to take me in his arms and kiss me. I burn with excitement remembering the night he kissed me, and I kissed him back. I take a deep breath to stop the warmth spreading through my cheeks. I curtsy and pop the tasty morsel into my mouth to hide the emotion seizing my body.

What's wrong? What is happening to me?

JOSEPH RETURNS FROM FILING THE PAPERS WITH the Fairfield County Superior Court in Bridgeport. After the judge interviews the girls, he appoints Joseph as their attorney. When he brings them back to the house, I assign the girls homework so that we can retire to my study.

"What's the next step?" I ask as soon as the door latches.

"The court has questions and concerns about the French demand for the return of the girls to France."

"I thought Captain Delacroix said we didn't have to worry until after the adoption's settled."

Joseph doesn't answer. Instead, he helps himself to one of my cigars. Before he lights it, he pours a snifter half full of brandy and takes a drink. Then, as if realizing that he's smoking my cigars and drinking my brandy, he says, "Would you like a brandy?"

"That would be nice." My words—my voice— drip with sarcasm.

He pours me a drink and, without so much as by your leave, takes up as if there had been no break in the conversation. He's oblivious of my exasperation at his ill-mannered behavior.

"He did, but he told us in a private conversation. The judge wants to hear it from him. There is no way we, or the court, can compel the appearance and testimony of a foreign diplomat."

"Diplomat? I thought he was an army lawyer."

"It seems our friend, Captain Julien Delacroix, is much more. He is the French military attaché. He may be a junior officer, but he is extremely well-placed in French politics. His father is the equivalent of one of our senators. An uncle is the head of the Ministry of War. Julien will someday be a general, mark my words."

"Invite him to dinner tomorrow. We'll ask him ourselves. I'm sure he'll help us."

"Don't get your hopes up. If Julien can help, he will. But if his orders are to the contrary, he will obey his superiors. I'll take the carriage into town and see if the good captain is available."

"I seem to be more concerned about the adoption and the intent of his government than you."

"Lura, I take everything involving you or your happiness seriously." He turns and storms from the house.

What's wrong with him? Have I done something to offend him or give him false hope? I did allow him to kiss me. What more does he expect?

An hour later, I find Earl in the kitchen, helping Cook polish the silver.

"Have you seen where Joseph has gone off to?"

"A few minutes ago, I saw him in the carriage house. He was hitching the sorrel. I offered to do it myself, but he declined, saying he wanted to be alone."

I walk to the carriage house intending to apologize, but Joseph's already gone. Why must he be so irritating? The more I'm around him, the more my feelings confuse me.

Could I be falling in love? No. I must not, I cannot. It's too soon.

JOSEPH MYER

I find Captain Delacroix relaxing in the shade of the hotel veranda. I'm in no mood for conversation. My head aches, and my teeth hurt. I've been grinding them since I left that prideful and hardheaded woman.

"Ah, Mr. Myer, to what do I owe the pleasure of your company on this fine afternoon? You must join me for a cigar and cognac."

If it were anyone but Julien, who I can't—must not—offend, I would give a polite no and walk on by, preferably to the bar and a stiff drink. I need this man on my side, at least to the extent possible in his position. I apologize for intruding. "Thank you for allowing me to interrupt what must be a busy schedule." He doesn't notice, or at least he pretends not to notice, my surly mood and the sullen tone in my words.

"Joseph, were that it was so, and as much as I enjoy Connecticut, there's not much here to keep me occupied. If not for a few of the people I have met, I would ask to be reassigned."

Remembering that she wants to have Julien to dinner, I soften my dour temperament. I enjoy his company and look forward to our chats. "We have a small way to help ease your boredom."

"How, Mon Ami?"

"First, I extend an invitation from Mrs. Myer to you. Please do her the honor of joining us for dinner at Grisham Manor tomorrow evening."

"That sounds pleasant. Will Miss Bartolini be there?"

"I'll stop by the mercantile on my way back to Grisham Manor and ask her to join us. Knowing you will be there will surely entice her to accept the invitation."

"Then you may tell Mrs. Myer that I'm enchanted to be her guest on the morrow."

"Julien, might I inquire as to your intentions regarding Miss Bartolini?"

"Is the personal life of a French officer and the owner of a business something you normally concern yourself with?"

"No, it's not. I consider you a friend. Otherwise, I would withhold any comment." I've offended Delacroix. "Forgive my discourtesy for addressing the matter with you, but Emily is a dear friend of Lura's. If she's hurt, Lura will suffer with her. I mean no offense."

"I assure you my intentions are honorable."

"Thank you, Julien. I appreciate your candor."

"Now, you must tell me what concerns you."

"You and Miss Bartolini differ in every aspect. You're a member of the French nobility, a man with a rich future, a handsome man who no doubt can attract the most beautiful of women. Am I wrong?"

"Modesty forbids me to agree, but I see your point. Emily is unlike me in most ways. In other ways, we are very much alike. She's an honest woman of many talents. Her father may have bestowed the mercantile upon her, but she has built it into a formidable business. Do you know she is opening a second store in Bridgeport?"

"No, I didn't. But then I'm not surprised at Emily's industriousness."

"Do you worry she is not what one might call a stylish woman, or that she's Italian?"

"It has crossed my mind."

"It is true that I have enjoyed an uncomplicated way with women and have known more than a few. None of those stylish or beautiful women have interested me for more than a fortnight. Emily intrigues me. I find her irresistible and wish to know her and her family. I don't know where this will lead, but if it were to end in marriage, I would not be disappointed."

"I'll not speak of it again."

"Bonne. Now is there something else that brought you here and occasioned the dinner invitation, Mon Ami."

"Yes, let me explain."

LURA MYER

"Welcome back to my home, Captain Delacroix. Thank you for being so gracious as to offer your carriage to Miss Bartolini. I hope it isn't too much of an inconvenience."

"None whatsoever, Lura. It is always a pleasure to join you and Joseph. Escorting Miss Bartolini adds to the joy of the event."

The girls have been waiting all day to see Emily. I promised them that if they dressed properly, they could join us for dinner. They appear suitably attired for young ladies attending an informal dinner party. Both are wearing below-the-knee bloused dresses with stockings, Ada Mae in pink and Katie in amber. Emily hugs them and whispers in their ears. I expect a disruption, "Emily, what mischief are you up to?"

With an impish grin, she tilts her head, feigns innocence, and says, "Why, Lura dearest, whatever do you mean?" My fear is confirmed—Emily is planning something. The girls are jumping up and down—something is afoot. As we take our seats, the girls rush to sit at each side of Emily. It appears Delacroix is in on the conspiracy as he smiles and takes his place between Ada Mae and me. I find myself flanked by him and Joseph, a quite pleasant arrangement.

After dessert, Emily, Ada Mae, and Katie retire to the girls' room, giving me a chance to question Julien about his intentions regarding the judge in Bridgeport. Julien tells us he has communicated the judge's request to his superiors at the Embassy in Washington.

"After I notified the ambassador of the court's request, he forwarded it to the Minister of Foreign Affairs in Paris. Thanks to the speed of the telegraph, I received an answer only hours before arriving here."

Although I've enjoyed an excellent meal, I have

an empty feeling in my stomach. While I clasp my pendant, Joseph clamps his hands together. I forget my manners as I say, "And?"

Captain Delacroix smiles and says, "I am permitted to speak with the judge regarding France's position in your case. There are limitations to what I may discuss and conditions on my appearance before an American court. I believe that if I meet those conditions, I shall satisfy the judge."

I can't control my elation as I release the pendant and clap my hands together. The warmth spreading throughout my body replaces the hollow ache in my stomach. I see a smile spreading across Joseph's face.

"Thank you, Julien. This means much to Joseph and me." Bending over, I kiss his cheek.

"Lura, if bringing good news wins such favor from you, I would deliver messages daily."

Smiling, I turn and hug Joseph.

Joseph and Julien retire to the study to enjoy a cigar and a brandy, while I make my way to the girls' bedchamber. At the foot of their beds are small valises. Picking one up, I say, "What's going on?"

"I've asked them if they would do me the honor of spending the night at my home. You can't refuse. I promise to return them after lunch tomorrow." Emily answers for the girls.

I try to be angry with Emily, but I've never managed to maintain that emotion with her. In an attempt to suggest irritation, I clasp my hands behind my back, raise my chin, and clench my jaw. It doesn't work.

"You're pretending to be angry." Emily laughs as she hugs me.

Trying to maintain control, I say in as stern a tone as I can muster, "I should be." I lose the moment and say, "But I'm not. I knew you were up to something when you conspired with the girls at dinner."

The girls are laughing and jumping up and down. Katie says, "Emily is going to give us each a new dress from her store. Isn't that grand?"

"Yes, it is, but you must not forget your lessons."

Ada Mae's the next to speak. "Emily will let me help her figure what people owe when they buy something. She says it's business arithmetic. She says someday, if it's alright with you, I can work in the store."

"Alright, alright. It's getting late, and you two young ladies need to be in bed soon. I'll ask Captain Delacroix if he'll give you a ride in his carriage."

Both girls speak at once. "Captain Delacroix already knows. He told Emily he would make room for us."

"Am I the only one who didn't know what you had planned?"

"Yes."

"So, even Joseph was part of your conspiracy."

"Well, we didn't tell him until before you brought the girls down to dinner."

JOSEPH MYER

Captain Delacroix agreed to an informal meeting with the judge. "Your Honor, may I present Captain Julien Delacroix of the French Army. Captain Delacroix is a member of the French Diplomatic Corps. As such, he isn't subject to the laws or orders of our government."

"Mr. Myer, I understand the captain's position vis-à-vis our laws. Captain, I appreciate your appearing here."

"It's my pleasure, Your Honor. I'm authorized to answer your questions, to a point. My government has placed certain restrictions on the way I answer. May we retire to your chambers?"

"I find your request highly unusual, but then, having a foreign diplomat in my court is quite rare." Rising from the bench, he says, "Gentlemen, let us retire to my chambers."

The judge opens a cigar box and invites Delacroix and me to join him. Once cigars are lit, we relax in comfortable chairs. The room is more like a study than an office.

"Captain, before we begin, would you please explain the restrictions you expect me to honor?"

"Your Honor, my government has strong feelings about the sovereignty of our nation and the sanctity of our laws. My instructions are to oppose any attempt you contemplate that doesn't coincide with our demands."

"What are your demands?"

"France has lodged a formal complaint with the American Embassy in Paris. We have demanded that Mrs. Myer return the girls, Catherine and Ada Mae Dean, to France and make herself available to answer criminal charges."

"Interesting, but I must ask you, Captain, do you believe our government will allow France to take two of our citizens in a case such as this? I doubt that Mrs. Myer will present herself to your country to answer what, under the circumstances, one might consider minor criminal charges."

"The answer to your first question is something that only emissaries of the highest order, American and French, can address. I would not presume to guess what they, in their wisdom, will ultimately decide. I'm at liberty to inform the court that until Mrs. Myer's petition to adopt the children is settled, my government will suspend any action or decision. Once Your Honor has approved or denied the petition for adoption, France will reexamine her position. More than that, I'm not at liberty to say."

"I understand what you've told me, Captain. Mr. Myer, do you have anything to add regarding the position of the French government?"

"No, sir, I don't, other than to say Captain Delacroix has been extraordinarily cooperative. My clients and I have nothing but the highest regard for him."

The judge takes a long pull on his cigar, leans toward Delacroix, and says, "Captain, if you don't mind, I have a few more questions."

"I will answer if able."

"Captain, you've been in Ridgefield for several weeks, is that correct?"

"Yes, sir."

"Have you come to know Mrs. Myer and the children in question?"

"Yes. I have found Mrs. Myer and the girls to be delightful."

"Good, good. In your opinion, would Mrs. Myer be a fit and caring mother to the girls?"

"Your Honor, I must object. Is that a proper question for you to ask outside the courtroom?" Joseph objects before Delacroix can answer.

"In normal circumstances, I would agree with you and withhold the question until the witness was under oath. In this instance, you've brought Captain Delacroix to me with the understanding that he will not be sworn in as a witness, and that I can only ask certain questions of him. Isn't that correct?"

"Yes, sir."

"Captain Delacroix has observed Mrs. Myer and the girls in their daily lives while under less than ideal conditions. You said you and your clients hold him in the highest regard. Is that not also correct?"

"Yes."

"Do you fear the captain will say something harmful to your petition?"

"No, sir, quite the contrary."

"Then, I shall ask him if he can answer the

question. Captain, would you like me to repeat the question?"

"No, sir. I would be pleased to answer if Mr. Myer has no further objection."

"I have none, Your Honor."

"Your Honor, I have come to know Mrs. Myer quite well in this brief period. I find her to be an honest woman of impeccable character. Her love for Katie and Ada Mae is undeniable. She cares for them as strongly as any mother could. The love she has for them is visible for all to see."

"Thank you, Captain. I have one final question for you. Have you formed an opinion about the girls and whether they would be happy if I grant the adoption?"

"Your Honor, Mr. Myer has informed me that the girls haven't had a mother in their life. Katie was two years old when their mother died. It's clear to me their father, Francis Dean, did everything a man could do to raise them to be fine young ladies." Delacroix seems to search for the right words before continuing. "I have observed the girls' behavior with Mrs. Myer. It is my opinion that they love her as much as she loves them. If adopted by Mrs. Myer, they will be happy and well cared for."

"I must apologize to you, Captain. Your comments have given rise to another question. If something should happen to Mrs. Myer, a widow, what would become of the girls?"

Joseph interrupts. "I believe I'm better qualified

to answer that question."

"Go ahead, Mr. Myer. I'm eager to hear what you have to say."

"As Your Honor knows, Mrs. Myer is an extremely wealthy woman. She intends to establish generous trust funds for both girls. Your Honor may not be aware, but Mrs. Myer's late husband was my half-brother. I'll be their uncle and will be there for them in the event some unfortunate malady overcomes Mrs. Myer."

"I didn't know, Mr. Myer. Thank you for telling me. Now, unless either of you has further information to present, you will excuse me. I must return to my courtroom. I have several other matters requiring my attention."

LURA MYER

When Joseph returns from Bridgeport, I send the girls off to the stables with Earl.

"What did Julien tell the judge?"

"Nothing different than what he has assured us. France will take no action until the adoption is settled."

"What did the judge say? How did he act? Is he favorable to my petition?" Lura asks in rapid-fire order.

"Lura, the judge appeared impartial. I don't think he has made up his mind. He shouldn't until he hears our petition in court. He had a few questions of

Julien about you and the girls."

"What did he want to know?"

"It's simple. The judge wanted to know if you loved the girls and if you would be a good mother."

"What did he tell him?"

"He told him you love the girls and would be a fine mother. He also said he believes the girls love you and would be happy to be your daughters. Now can we eat?"

"THE JUDGE HAS NOTIFIED ME THAT HE'LL HEAR the adoption petition in three weeks," Joseph announces with a flourish.

The news that we have a date for the hearing is both wonderful and frightening. As fall approaches, I can't help but recall the trials and tribulations of the previous year. I pray that 1894 ends much more happily for the girls and me.

Father once took me to the courthouse in Bridgeport. The old courthouse was built of wood. The harsh Connecticut winters required several fireplaces located on the ground floor with outlets for heat on the second level. Another was housed in the basement. When the court was in session, a handyman kept busy servicing the fires. In 1888, he decided upon a plan to reduce his effort. Once the fires were going well, he placed enough wood in each to fill the burning chamber. Before he reached the ground floor fireplace, the wood in the basement spilled out, and soon, the entire building was engulfed in flames.

The town elders, fearful of losing courthouse business to another town, hastily made plans to replace the old building. Several ideas were under consideration when word reached the elders about a similar situation in Litchfield County. Their court-house burned to the ground and was replaced with another wood structure. This second building burnt to the ground before it was dedicated.

The Bridgeport elders commissioned Robert Wakeman Hill of Waterbury to design and build a courthouse of stone. Hill completed the Litchfield County courthouse and then one of similar design in Bridgeport. Father took me to the dedication of the new Bridgeport courthouse in 1890. Now, four years later, I'm back. The edifice is an imposing structure facing the city square. A large clock dominates the bell tower, with its cold and stark stone walls. The courtroom is impressive with twenty-foot ceilings, the judge's bench set on a raised platform. The top is piled high with books and papers, creating an opening through which the judge can oversee the lawyers and visitors.

"Lura, sit here in the front row with the girls. When the judge calls our case, the three of you should remain here until I call you to testify. How do you feel?"

"I'm fine, and the girls are as well. We have Emily, Mr. Bartolini, and Julien here if we find the need for help. I thought Mr. Brandeis would be here."

"Louis is on his way. I understand there was a derailment between here and New York. I'm sure as soon as he gets beyond the hazard, he'll be here."

Joseph turns his attention to the girls. "Katie, how are you this morning?"

"Uncle Joseph, you told me what to do, but I forgot. I'm scared."

"It's okay to be nervous. Everyone feels that way in a courthouse. I'm sure even Miss Lura is a little scared."

I'm fearful. I give Joseph a look that tells him he isn't helping. I pull Katie close and whisper in her ear, "Don't mind Joseph, he doesn't know everything. If you get scared, hold me tight."

Joseph has one final question for each of the girls. "Katie, this is the day of the adoption. If the court grants our petition, you will be Lura's daughter, Catherine Margaret Dean Myer. The judge will ask you if that's what you want."

"Oh, Uncle Joseph, I want that more than anything. I love Miss Lura and want to be her daughter."

Joseph smiles and hugs Katie. He repeats the question, getting a similar answer from Ada Mae. After hugging her, he proceeds to the front of the courtroom and takes a seat. Turning, he whispers that our case won't be heard until after the other lawyers have their hearings.

The morning drags on for what seems like a fortnight. After the judge finishes with the other cases, the marshal steps up to the bench. They converse for a few minutes before the marshal leaves the courtroom. The judge doesn't look pleased.

"Mr. Myer, please approach the bench."

While Joseph's listening to the judge, Mr. Brandeis sits down next to me. "Good day, Mrs. Myer." He points to Joseph and says, "What's going on? I thought our hearing would start long before this late hour."

"I don't know. We were about to be called when the marshal came in and rushed up to the judge. When the marshal left, he called Joseph up. They've been talking for a good five minutes or more."

It's another five minutes before Joseph steps back. As he does, the judge hits his gavel on the desk and says, "Court is adjourned until two o'clock. Mr. Myer, I expect you to be ready to proceed when court resumes."

"Yes, sir. We'll be ready. Mr. Brandeis has arrived and will be joining me at the counsel table."

TWENTY-SIX

JOSEPH MYER

We had decided Louis would examine Lura, but when we returned from lunch, she said to Louis, "If you don't mind, I would feel much better if Joseph questioned me today. I can't explain it, but that's my wish."

Louis says, "That's an excellent idea, Mrs. Myer." I'm surprised when he says nothing further about the matter.

"Bailiff, call the matter of Ada Mae Dean and Catherine Margaret Dean."

I open the small gate and usher the girls and Lura to chairs next to Louis and me. "Sit here, ladies."

I've represented hundreds of clients over the years, but I've never been so personally involved in a matter. It's a warm summer day, but I shiver from an unexplained chill. My stomach is in turmoil. I fear I'll be sick. I must control myself. Lura and the girls are depending on me.

"Who represents the interests of the children?"

"I do. Joseph Myer assisted by Mr. Louis Brandeis." Taking a deep breath, the chill leaves me. My stomach relaxes.

"It's an honor to have you in our humble courtroom, Mr. Brandeis. Welcome," the judge says to Louis.

"The honor is mine. Thank you."

"Who represents Mrs. Lura Myer in this matter?"

"I do Your Honor, with the assistance of Mr. Brandeis."

"Fine, let's begin. I've read the petition. I find it to be in order. Mr. Myer, do you have any additional evidence or witnesses to present?"

"No, Your Honor."

"Do your younger clients understand what's transpiring here today?"

"Yes, sir, they do."

"Mr. Myer, I wish to examine your clients. Please have the elder child, I believe Ada Mae Dean, take the stand."

"This is where you sit in that chair, and the judge will ask you some questions," I say while pointing to the witness seat. "When he finishes, I may ask you a few more. Are you ready?"

When Ada Mae takes the stand, she looks small, dwarfed by the size of a chair designed for grownups.

The judge surprises me. Instead of having her swear on a Bible, he speaks to her in a gentle tone. "Good day, Ms. Dean."

"Good day."

"Well, Miss Dean, is it alright if I call you Ada Mae?"

Twisting and fidgeting, she flattens her dress by pushing down and away before answering. "Yes, sir."

"Are you frightened?" With eyes large, she shakes her head up and down while biting her lip. "You don't need to be. I want to find out if you want to go home with Mrs. Myer."

"I want to be with Miss Lura."

"Fine. I need to ask you a few questions. Do you know the difference between the truth and a lie?"

"Yes, sir. I must always tell the truth. A lie is bad, and my papa told me liars go to hell."

The judge smiles at her and continues. "I think we can assume Miss Dean will truthfully answer our questions. Ada Mae, do you understand what it means to be adopted?"

"If Miss Lura adopts us, me and Katie, we will be her daughters and live with her forever."

"Do you want to be adopted by Mrs. Myer?"

"Yes sir, I want to be Miss Lura's daughter, so does Katie."

"Mr. Myer, do you or Mr. Brandeis have any questions of this witness?"

"No, Your Honor."

"Have the younger child take the stand."

The only difference between the questions the judge has for Katie is when he asks her if she's frightened. In a strong, clear voice, she says, "No, I'm not."

When the judge finishes, neither Louis nor I have any questions for Katie.

It's time for Lura to take the stand. The judge asks, "Do you swear to tell the truth, the whole truth, and nothing but the truth so help you God?"

"Yes, sir, I do." Her answer is loud and clear.

"Your Honor," I stand, "if it pleases the court, I would like to question the witness."

"You may begin your examination of Mrs. Myer."

"Mrs. Myer, would you explain to the court how the children came to be in your care?"

Lura's voice quivers for the first few minutes of her testimony, and then she settles down. Turning in the witness chair, she addresses the judge directly. In ten minutes or less, she ends with, "And that's how I came to love these girls."

The judge has no questions and excuses her. "Thank you, Mrs. Myer. You may step down."

Once Lura returns to her seat, the judge glances at his notes before looking up. It's as if he notices Delacroix for the first time. "Captain Delacroix. Welcome. I'm glad to see you here today."

"Your Honor?" Delacroix stands at attention.

"Captain, please be at ease. I don't intend to put you at a disadvantage, but can you tell me if your government's position has changed since we last we spoke."

"No, sir, it has not." Julien doesn't look at all uncomfortable.

"Thank you, Captain."

Returning to his notes, the judge frowns as he taps his gavel against a stack of papers. His gaze wanders to some secret spot over the door at the rear of the chamber. After what seems like minutes, but is only seconds, he shakes his head as if awakening from a dream. "The court will take a brief recess. Mr. Myer, Mr. Brandeis, please join me in chambers."

This time there's no offer of a cigar. The judge sits behind his desk and gestures for us to sit. He's quiet. Finally, "Gentlemen, I'm having a great deal of difficulty deciding this matter."

"Don't you believe Mrs. Myer loves and wants to care for the children?"

"That isn't my problem, Mr. Myer, I have no doubt she loves the children and that they love her."

"I'm confused. Your Honor, if you believe they love each other and she can provide for them, what's your concern?"

"Mrs. Myer is a widow, a single woman. Precedent in Connecticut dictates a child will be adopted by two parents, a mother, and a father."

This is the one precedent in Connecticut law that has bothered me since my visit to the law library in the basement of this building.

"Mrs. Myer isn't your typical widow. She's an

educated woman of the world, and she may well be the third or fourth wealthiest woman in America. If there ever was a time for breaking precedent, this is it," Louis says.

"I don't disagree. Mrs. Myer is all that and more. I fear that someone could dispute my decision and take it up on appeal. I don't want to see my decision overturned. If she were married, I would have no qualms. I would grant the petition at once."

Both Louis and I object to no avail. The one concession the judge grants us is to stay his decision for forty-eight hours. I point out to him that would require a decision on Saturday. After a more strenuous argument, he agrees to withhold judgment until the following Monday.

"Gentlemen, please return to the courtroom. I'll be there presently. I wish to review a case decision."

Lura can see by our expressions something is amiss. I decide that now isn't a suitable time to articulate what the judge has said. I tell her that the judge will make his decision on Monday.

THE CARRIAGE RIDE BACK TO RIDGEFIELD IS strained. Even the girls are subdued. Leaving Louis at his hotel, we continue to Grisham Manor. For once, I'm glad that Emily and Delacroix are traveling in their carriage. Neither Lura nor I are in the mood for company. I try to engage her in conversation, but shaking her finger in my face, she snaps, "There's something you're not telling me. Until you're ready to speak, I wish to be alone with my thoughts."

I'm angry at the judge, but I refuse to allow it to show. Lura means too much to the girls and me. I must overcome his hesitancy and convince him to approve the adoption. If I lose this case, it will be more than the case I lose. I'll lose this woman who I've come to admire. I'm in love with her.

As we pull to a halt under the portico, Lura throws the carriage door open with such force it slams against the side. The girls wait until she has entered the house before alighting. Inside, she seems somewhat calmer. In a controlled voice, hollow and stilted, she says, "Please come to the study." She gives me no chance to answer before turning and walking away. The girls look at me with questions in their eyes.

Earl appears. "Mr. Joseph, I'll take the girls. Ada Mae, Katie, come. Cook is baking and could use your help."

"Thank you, Earl."

I find Lura sitting behind her father's desk. She's stiff, rigid, with her chin drawn in. My Lord, she looks formidable.

"Lura."

"Don't tell me. I'm to lose the girls. Please . . ."

The facade disappears, and she cries. I rush to her. I want to take her into my arms. Instead, I place one hand on her shoulder and utter false assurances.

"Tell me the truth. Stop trying to protect me. All

you're doing is making this more difficult."

After I explain what the judge said, Lura's apoplectic, "Because I'm a widow? That's his justification? The man is a coward."

"Yes, that's true. The Judge is afraid of being reversed on appeal. However, the decision is in his hands."

"There has to be something we can do. Can you appeal his decision?"

"Yes," I hesitate, "we can appeal his decision, but that could take years. You could probably care for the girls during the process, but you might have to give them up eventually."

"There has to be a way around this. Joseph, you must have an idea. What can we do?"

"Yes, there's a way around his objection," I say after the briefest hesitancy.

"Tell me."

"It has long been the custom for a man to marry his brother's widow and care for her and any children. I would be honored if you would allow me to become your husband."

Standing, Lura slaps me, drops her hand, and barks, "Honor? That might be an honor for you, but I would never marry any man from some false sense of honor. I will marry for love or not at all."

She raises her hand to slap me a second time. I grab her arms and hold her away from me. "Lura, I love you, and you love me."

She stiffens, and for an instant, I think she's

going to pull away. She doesn't. Her resistance fades as she looks into my eyes.

"Do you love me?"

"With all my heart and soul."

EPILOGUE

IN 1901, EARL AND COOK RETIRE AND MARRY. THEY live out their lives in the home Walter Myer built and which Lura gave them as a wedding gift.

May 1, 1915, *Général de brigade* Julien Delacroix dies a horrific death when the Germans use poison gas during the Second Battle of Ypres. He leaves behind his Italian-American wife, Emily, and their two children, a boy and a girl.

In 1916, Louis Brandeis becomes an Associate Justice of the United States Supreme Court despite strong Republican opposition. He serves with distinction for twenty-two years.

In 1920, Joseph Myer enters politics at the suggestion of his friend, Justice Brandeis. Elected to the U.S. Senate, he dies six months into his first term. One week after being diagnosed with cancer of the liver, he breathes his last breath.

The children grown, Lura Myer, twice widowed, lives her remaining years at Grisham Manor. She dies in 1950 at the age of eighty.

About the Author

George Cramer lives in Dublin, California, with his wife, Cathy. They have four adult children.

When his career in law enforcement ended, due to multiple line-of-duty injuries, a second career in private and corporate investigations took him in a new and equally challenging direction.

Mr. Cramer left the corporate environment where he last worked as the head of Global Investigations, Safety & Security for the Palm, Inc. Division of Hewlett-Packard. He specialized in Standards of Business Conduct, undercover operations; insurance and corporate fraud; crimes against business; and the protection of intellectual property.

He is recognized as an expert in the area of Interviewing and Interrogation and has presented numerous seminars, including at ASIS-International and High Technology Crime Investigators international conferences.

George Cramer's love of writing and the English language resulted in his return to college, where he earned two additional degrees. One in English and a Master of Fine Arts/Creative Writing – Fiction at the Institute of American Indian Arts.

He is currently working on two projects, a thriller spanning forty years, and a modern-day police procedural.

CPSIA information can be obtained
at www.ICGtesting.com
Printed in the USA
FSHW012331191221
87042FS